paper
advertising
collectibles

paper advertising collectibles

Treasures from Almanacs to Window Signs

by Robert Reed

ATB

ANTIQUE TRADER BOOKS

A Division of Landmark
Specialty Publications
Norfolk, Virginia

This book is dedicated to Claudette Swengel Reed, my partner, pal, and playmate.

ISBN: 0-930625-91-9
Library of Congress Catalog Card Number: 98-72115

Managing Editor: Allan W. Miller
Editor: Sandra Holcombe
Graphic Designer: Chris Decker

Printed in the United States of America

For a complete catalog of Antique Trader Books and to
learn more about our other publications for collectors,
please contact:

Antique Trader Publications
P.O. Box 1050
Dubuque, Iowa 52004
1-800-334-7165

contents

BUY AN INTEREST IN YOUR COUNTRY
BUY DEFENSE BONDS AND STAMPS-NOW!
WORLD HEAVYWEIGHT CHAM
HOLYFIE
TYSON
NOV. 8, 199
9PM ET/6PM
N PAY-PER-V
TVKO
NE DAY ONLY)
5 7:30 9:30
Person
DIRECT FROM H
HUNTZ
"SACH"
HALL
AND
GABE
DELL
STARS OF
THE "BOWERY BOYS"
THE ORIGINAL
"DEAD END K
TIME IS SLIPP
TRAVEL NOW!
It's Cheaper than Staying Home
SEE SCHULT TRAILERS BEFORE YOU BUY
ANY PLACE IS HOME IN A SCHULT TRAILER
ne tim
is now

acknowledgments

Please allow my deep appreciation to all those who helped make this book possible. My greatest gratitude, of course, goes to my photographer (and wonderful wife), Claudette Reed, who provided 90 percent of the illustrations for this book and about 110 percent of the inspiration.

Also, a special tribute is due to the antique malls and shops everywhere which were also so helpful, but particularly the Knightstown (IN) Antique Mall, Lindon's Antique Mall, Heartland, and Sugar Creek Antique Mall, where the owners and staff remain eternally kind and helpful.

Special appreciation and thanks additionally to Antique and Collectible News Service, Cohasco (historical documents auctions), Cerebro (tobacco ephemera auctions), Leland's Collectibles (sports memorabilia auctions), Hake's Americana & Collectibles (mail and phone auctions), Skinner, Inc. (auctioneers and appraisers), and Swann Galleries (book and ephemera auctions). Addresses and numbers of these firms are listed on this book's resources page.

chapter one
introduction

Paper advertising. There is a lot of it out there. If there were not a wealth of everything from almanacs to window signs still to be found and claimed, there would be little point in putting this book together. If museums or landfills held all the treasures printed on paper which have praised products and services, there would be little reason to read on.

The fact is we have only really just begun to find any value in paper advertising collectibles. For the most part, we collectively just tossed them aside. Their original purpose was, after all, to be relatively short-lived. Their message was to buy, rent, subscribe, participate, obey, or otherwise respond to what was usually (but not always) a commercial venture. Beyond the message, they were unimportant. Unlike most antiques and collectibles, paper advertising usually never entered the world with any real status.

But wait. We threw away all those catalogs, calendars, advertising fans, posters, ink blotters, and handbills. That's what everybody was supposed to do, right? Looking back, some of those magazine ads and political bumper stickers were kind of neat, if not even a little bit historic. So didn't anybody save any of that stuff?

The answer is: Not really—not at the time—not in any organized way.

Frankly, most of the paper advertising from the past which has survived has done so because no one got around to throwing it away—and a great deal of that is still out there.

One of the first glimpses that Americans had of paper advertising came in colonial newspapers. In the beginning, newspapers sought to be more literary than commercial, but they gradually saw the economic advantage of paid messages.

In early 1704, printer and publisher John Campbell announced that his newly purchased *Boston News-Letter* would now accept a certain amount of advertising:

"Persons who have any Houses, Lands, Tenements, Farms, Ships, Vessels, Goods, Wares or Merchandise, to be Sold or Let; or Servants Runaway, or Goods Stole or Lots; may have the same inserted at a Reasonable rate."

In the very next issue, Campbell himself advertised, offering a reward for the return of two iron anvils, weighing between 120 and 140 pounds each. They had been lost off "Mr. Shippen's Wharff," and a reward was offered for their return.

Except for headlines, advertisements in colonial newspapers were frequently set up like regular reading matter, according to James Lee, author of *The History of American Journalism.*

"They were usually small in size, and not infrequently limited in size by the printer," adds Lee. "Strange as it may seem, however, these advertisements when read today are

Bellows maker's trade sign, illustrated in 1826 newspaper ad from Boston.

almost as interesting as the text. They tell a story which needs little by way of interpretation."

One good example was provided by a woman named Deliverance who ran her own "classified" advertisement in a 1734 issue of the *New York Gazette*. She may have been one of the first of her gender to use such advertising, and undoubtedly was an early advocate of women's rights as well:

"Whereas James Moor of Woodbridge has advertised in this *Gazette*, as well as by Papers sent out and posted up, that his Wife, Deliverance, has eloped from his Bed and Board. These are to certifie, that the Same is altogether false, for She has lived with Him above Eight Years under His Tyranny and incredible Abuses, for He has several times attempted to murder Her and also turned Her out of Doors, shamefully abusing Her, which is well known to the Neighbors and Neighbourhood in Woodbridge."

For the most part, these early ads dealt with goods shipped to local merchants, or books and pamphlets produced by local printers; however, even the legendary Benjamin Franklin used them on occasion for personal messages. He ran the following ad around 1740 in the *Pennsylvania Gazette*:

"Taken out of Pew in the Church some months since, a Common Prayer Book, bound in red, gilt, and lettered D.F. (for Deborah Franklin) on each cover. The Person who took it is desired to open it and read the eighth Commandment, and afterwards return it into the same Pew again, upon which no further Notice will be taken."

By the 1750s, that same newspaper was running advertisements from merchants that included imported items as diverse as men's and women's thread. For the most part, however, newspaper advertising remained unchanged until well into the nineteenth century when woodcut illustrations became a common addition to the advertising format.

In 1826, a bellows maker's ad was illustrated with the object which was manufactured and sold. It served the same purpose as the trade sign which hung above the shop's door, and was, in fact, a drawing of the same sign. The

Busy drugstore shown in an Oregon newspaper ad sketch from 1862.

advertisement proudly added the location, "at the sign of the Bellows, No. 276, Ann Street, Boston." In the 1860s, an Oregon newspaper provided an illustration of a busy (and apparently prosperous) drugstore that offered everything from artists' tools to patent medicines. The Smith and Davis drugstore was billed in the ad as the largest on the Pacific Coast. During the same period, in the Midwest, a photographer's newspaper ad included the sketch of a camera in hopes of luring customers to the studio. In 1879, a striking ad featured the detailed drawing of a horse-drawn hearse. The undertaker promised, "Our prices are as low as any other first-class establishment in the west."

With all their diversity and distribution, though, newspapers were not the only form of paper advertising used in the country's early days. Broadsides (the forerunner of posters) and handbills were frequently put into service to inform and perhaps to influence the public (at least the public that could read).

Typically, a broadside, which is sometimes referred to as a broadsheet, was printed on one side of a large sheet of paper. The size of the paper was often determined by the capacity of the available press. For the most part, broadsides of the eighteenth century were legal notices which were required by law to be published. A 1781 broadside proclaimed depreciation rates on contracts enacted in Massachusetts. The rates had actually been enacted some four years earlier. An "Address to Drunkards" was published via broadside in 1795 as an Indian Letter. It was issued in Boston and was based on a letter from Captain Hendricks, an Indian Chief of the Stockbridge nation. It warned, "our enemy is named rum." The 8" x 11" sheet brought $1,495 at a Skinner's Inc. auction in Boston during the latter part of 1996.

The trend in broadside usage in the United States during the 1700s and early 1800s was largely to alert citizens about special events, new regulations, governmental and political meetings, fundraising lotteries for projects like canals, and sometimes even social events. It was not unusual for patriotic songs to be posted as broadsides. Naturally, those broadsheets that are related to the American

Photographic artist ad in a local newspaper during the Civil War.

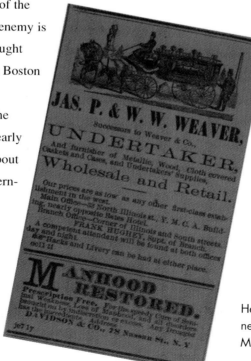

Hearse illustrated in 1879 newspaper ad for a Midwestern undertaker.

Revolution are the most prized today and can bring thousands of dollars at major auctions.

Moving into the second quarter of the nineteenth century and beyond, the broadside, besides being a message center for all levels of government from federal to local, also bore an increasing number of commercial messages or advertisements, if you will. In 1849, Salem Coach used a broadside to advertise new coach routes in Massachusetts. Printed by the *Salem Gazette Press*, the broadsides were even illustrated with pointing fingers and stagecoaches. A 20" x 14" broadside advertising the Concord Grape was published and distributed in 1856 around Concord, Massachusetts. It was aptly illustrated with an attractive group of grapes.

Eventually, broadsides gave way to the somewhat more elaborately printed posters, although the term was not generally used until late in the nineteenth century. Some accounts say posters began to have a separate identity once color was used on them rather than the traditional black and white design.

In some few cases, broadsides were printed on both sides so they could be folded for distribution. Generally, however, smaller sheets known as handbills were used for double-side printing and then "handed" out to individuals, usually at busy public places. Handbills of Colonial days were more often than not 8 1/2" x 14", but a 9" x 12" size was more common after the 1840s. Handbills enjoyed a very long life in terms of paper advertising; they remained popular throughout the nineteenth century and well into the twentieth century.

Interestingly, still another form of paper advertising—trade cards—made an impact on Colonial America after being imported from England where they were even more popular. During the eighteenth and early nineteenth centuries, they remained little more than finely printed business cards, with a bit of illustration. In New York City, furniture maker William Buttre adapted a two-

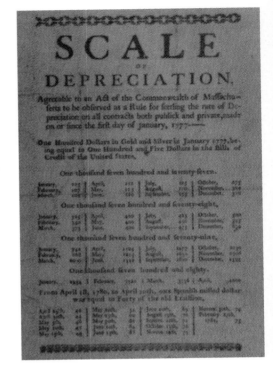

Broadside, 1781, proclaiming depreciation rates on contracts enacted by Massachusetts.

Broadside on drunkeness posted as Indian Letter, ca. 1795, "Our enemy is named rum." (Skinner Inc. auction photo)

Salem Coach advertising broadside printed in July of 1849. (Skinner Inc. auction photo)

scene trade card around 1813 which included an illustration from the workplace. A few years earlier, the enterprising Buttre had used a woodcut of a fancy chair on printed billheads, as well as to advertise his business in a section of the New York City directory. Today, an example of his early trade card is part of the archives at Winterthur Museum at Winterthur, Delaware.

After nearly a century of being a very selective means of advertising, trade cards were quite enthusiastically re-discovered during the Victorian era, thanks mainly to vastly improved printing techniques and a robust demand. They became one of the very few paper advertising collectibles to be immediately collected by the general public.

Catalogs, too, had a significant role in commerce by the last quarter of the nineteenth century. Generally, the boom in industrial productivity following the Civil War and during the 1870s meant that merchants on the "frontier" had to depend on warehouses back East. Likewise, customers were often forced to depend on a growing number of mail-order supply houses. The result was a flood of trade catalogs providing everything from firearms and hardware, to garden seeds and farm equipment. Ultimately, with their vast selections, detailed prices, and capturing illustrations, they became a fine art of paper advertising as well.

In this volume are presented special sections on the main categories of paper advertising collectibles. The reader can take an even closer look at almanacs, calendars, catalogs, fans, ink blotters, advertising in magazines, political advertising on paper, advertising postcards, posters, signs, and trade cards. Also included is an "everything else" chapter dealing with smaller areas of paper advertising such as billheads, booklets, handbills, labels, product containers, and promotional road maps.

Hopefully, the reader will go beyond what is presented in this book, and gain new insight into the field of advertising paper collectibles. The opportunities for collecting paper advertisements are great. There is, as I have previously noted, a lot out there.

Broadside advertising *The Concord Grape*, printed in Concord, Mass., 1856. (Skinner Inc. auction photo)

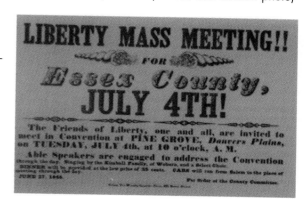

Broadside for Fourth of July meeting, dated 1848, Massachusetts. (Skinner Inc. auction photo)

chapter two
the future as it looked in the past

*"If you want the present to be different
from the past, study the past."*
Baruch Spinoza, 1600s

During my early days as a young reporter for a small weekly newspaper, I spent a great deal of time at a beautiful and immense old courthouse. The nineteenth century building was mammoth and solid, but no longer large enough for a rapidly growing community. One morning on my rounds, I was greeted by a public official who told me in fairly salty language that a large room near the top of the structure was about to be cleaned out to make room for more county records.

"We're getting rid of everything in that room," he confided. "The county commissioners have been on my back for more space, so all that old stuff goes." (For the record, Mr. Salty didn't call it "stuff" either.)

The official invited me to take a farewell look. As it turned out, it was an enormous chamber of a room, with 12-foot high marble ceilings. Every nook and cranny was jammed with documents, bill-heads, broadsides, letters, ledger books, posters, trade catalogs, court orders, public notices, and various other paper detailing that particular county's business transactions during most, if not all, of the nineteenth century. Not only were all the vast

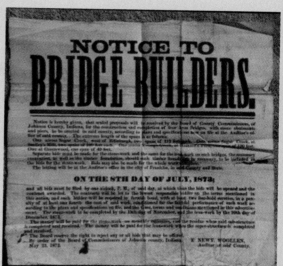

Notice to Bridge Builders broadside posted in 1873 by county officials.

shelves and boundless tables overflowing with dusty records and material, but the floor itself was at least six-inches deep in most places with paper of all types. To me, at the time, it was all fairly dark and musty, and certainly no great place to be.

"They're due to shovel it all out today," continued the official with a growing sense of accomplishment, "It's all going to the dump." Idly, I reached down to pick up a hand-ful of the papers, and thrust them into my jacket pocket. I thought, at the time, I would do a little story on the courthouse clean-up, but, as it turned out, there was so much other news going on that week that I never got around to the big "clean up and make room" story. Years later, I heard—off-the-record, of course—that the ambitious official probably should have kept at least some of the documents for future reference, or at least delegated some of it to the local historical society. What he did may even have been illegal. But at that point in time, the public official had long since gone on to that great courthouse in the sky, and he certainly was not accountable to mere county authorities, much less the local historical society. I never wrote about, nor even really mentioned, the incident in the years that followed. Not long after the encounter at the courthouse, I even tossed out the aged paper examples. Like the official, I was cleaning out my desk at the newspaper office to make room for other "stuff" of seemingly greater importance.

Basically, the same thing happened on a greater scale throughout the United States during World War II. In 1944, one of the most successful paper scrap drives of the war was conducted under the direction of federal government officials. The cause was great, and everyone pitched in to throw away about every scrap of paper they could find. People were so anxious to help the war effort of course, and really did not think anything in the attic, closet, or garage needed to be saved. "Consequently," concluded one journalist just a few years later, "the value thrown away in the trash drive may have approximated the total value of the new paper that was made from all that scrap. Several million dollars worth of rich and rare stuff was in that new paper."

A tiny example could be found in New York City. A prosperous old firm dating back to the 1840s decided to empty its files of old paper—including a great deal of advertising materials. In keeping with the patriotic drive, they bundled up the vast accumulation and notified a junk dealer. As fate would have it, a reporter (apparently not as busy as I had been on the county courthouse beat), picked up on the account and wrote a brief story. At another location in the city, a bookseller read the story and immediately called the firm to see if the deal was already done. It was. Undiscouraged, the bookseller hailed a taxi and rode to the site of the junk dealer's operation. Joy in the morning, most of the old paper was still there! Our bookseller pulled out several hundred pounds of it, for which he happily paid the junk dealer $25 for the opportunity. Within 24 hours, the bookseller had sold just a small group of the items to a leading educational institution for $500.

The truth is, we have been seriously trashing paper in general (and paper advertising in particular) ever since the first label of a Colonial cabinetmaker was slapped on a chest of drawers, and since the poster of the next town hall event was calmly pasted over last week's big announcement. (So pleased to have the original label of highly regarded New York cabinetmaker Michael Allison intact and in good shape, the University of the State of New York included it in a major exhibit of furniture back in 1988.)

Cabinetmaker's paper label, ca. 1800, M. Allison with some advertising. (University of New York)

It comes as no real surprise, then, that for much of the twentieth century experts in the fields of antiques and collectibles held little regard for paper advertising. Even as late as the 1960s, Warman's *Eighth Edition of Antiques and Their Prices* took small note of such things. Posters, catalogs, cardboard signs, and trade cards were not mentioned. An unspecified advertising fan was listed with a retail price of $1.50. Neither the date nor the advertiser were included in the listing. Warman's, however, at the time a leading publication in the price guide field, did list almanacs. The highest price for an almanac was $15 for a 1776 issue of the *North American Almanac*, by Samuel Stearns. Following the listed almanacs was a notation that most published after 1880 sold for $1 each. The publication also included a small listing of catalogs, including the 1902 Sears and Roebuck issue, and a few other general mail-order catalogs such as Butler Brothers, Montgomery Ward and Company, and Macy's. A few nineteenth century women's magazines also merited mention in the guide.

In 1965, Lawrence Romaine provided a chapter on trade catalogs for *The Concise Encyclopedia of American Antiques*. Romaine recommended saving catalogs which were the number one issue, those offering new designs and models representing the nation's expansion, and better illustrated wholesale catalogs; howev-

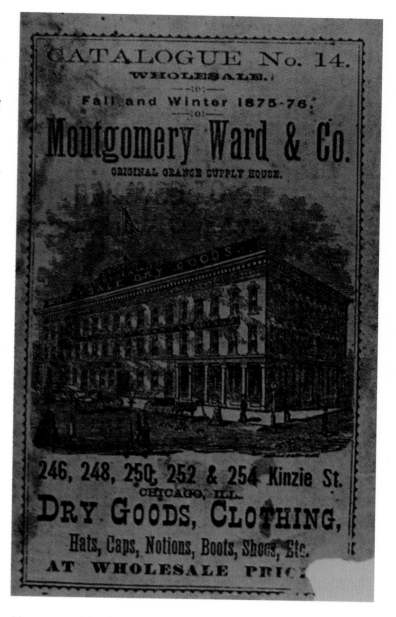

Montgomery Ward & Company catalogue, 1875-1876. Wholesale prices from Chicago.

er, even the noted expert warned against trying to collect them all. "A complete accumulation under any one heading would be practically impossible," said Romaine. "I do not suggest that even the Library of Congress should try to preserve them." And, Romaine added, "There is no practical method of appraising the standards of future (trade catalog) collecting." Not much more hopeful was John Mebane, the highly successful author of numerous books on the emerging attraction of antiques and collectibles during the 1960s.

"There are very few specialists in this field of listing and selling early American trade catalogs, but those few know their catalog values," said Mebane. The author warned, however, that "a number of amateurs, noting the seeming high prices of cata-

Corn planter featured on trade card from Vandivier Corn Planter Company, 1880s.

logs, have recently plunged into the stream without knowing how to swim, and are asking outrageous prices for commonplace catalogs in plentiful supply, unaware apparently that the value of a trade catalog depends upon more than its being just a catalog." Mebane, writing in the book, *Treasure at Home*, added two other points regarding catalogs. One was that the best market for those selling catalogs from the past might well be "institutions which already possess collections," museums, and various historical societies. Secondly, persons who insist on mint copies of all catalogs they buy are not acting with the greatest wisdom, and are probably passing up many highly desirable catalogs they won't have an opportunity to locate again.

Mebane had some more things to say about paper advertising collectibles back in the 1960s. In one of his many books, he observed a tendency to acquire old scrapbooks which had been filled with "trade and advertising cards, early automobile advertisements, old labels, admission tickets, and similar material." These, along with lithographed letterheads depicting buildings and other early typography, were just in the early stages of collectibility, according to Mebane. "Since many of these items are really just beginning to be collected, their values are not high," he pointed out. "Nevertheless, they are high enough to make them worth acquiring, and perhaps holding, in anticipation of increased value within the next decade." Interestingly, he was much more positive about posters. "Some of today's most artistic posters will undoubtedly be collectors' items in years to come," he flatly (and accurately) forecast in his 1966 book, *New Horizons in Collecting*.

Site of sale paper sign, made by Strobridge & Co. Lithograph of Cincinnati, Ohio, ca. 1880s.

Not many other books or periodicals were that prophetic during the 1960s. Some spoke of a growing interest in broadsides, posters, and handbills, but largely as a pastime for bookdealers and not a serious area for the rest of the business field. Trade cards were also given mention on occasion, but more as an interesting way to keep track of commercial and social development, and rarely as a valued investment.

Things changed somewhat in the 1970s. Many general price guides began paying attention to paper collectibles, and a few specialized books devoted specifically to the subject began to appear. *The Official Guide to Paper Americana,* by Hal Cohen, for example, noted in 1972 that some trade cards, including those with sports, early autos, famous Americans, early trains, bicycles, balloons, and clipper ships had significant value. Further, Cohen observed that, generally, prices on all types of early trade catalogs had risen, especially Sears, Montgomery Ward, Johnson Smith, and Butler Brothers. He also cited growing interest in such specialized categories for catalogs as glassware, jewelry, toys, furniture, and automobiles. Finally, he foresaw a wonderful future for advertising posters. "The present popularity of the American poster more than compensates for their former neglect," he noted. "Enthusiasts will frame a tattered poster today in the same spirit our ancestors encased an old fragment of worn lace." Cohn centered on war, movie, and advertising posters and concluded that, "the affinity between old posters and today's pop art is apparent to the casual observer. Consequently, they not only blend with a traditional setting, but also enhance a modern decor."

Colorful cover of Kellogg's trade magazine for dealers in the early 1900s, full color.

Box-shaped JELL-O folder, early twentieth century.

Gradually, paper advertising collectibles have become more and more relevant to the social order of things and the collecting field. Not surprisingly, they have been listed more and more frequently in popular price guides and trade publications, and yet not all accounts have been with profound insight and wisdom. As late as the early 1990s, some price guides were proclaiming that old magazines (apparently even those with prized advertisements in them) were still nearly worthless and not worth saving. For all the clarity of Morgan Towne, Lawrence Romaine, John Mebane, and a few others, there was an army of undistinguished and uninformed non-believers who concluded that as long as we were happily throwing it away with both hands, it would never ever prove to be anything worthwhile, much less actually collectible.

chapter three
advertising almanacs

Almanacs offer a faded glory. Part of their appeal is the fact that they have come and gone on the American scene. Like a great aunt of family legends, it is possible to reflect on their life from beginning to end, and wonder about the times in which they thrived. With all due respect to the *Old Farmer's Almanac* and a few others, the almanac is no longer a part of the culture of this country. While more of us can read than ever before, we no longer thumb through the almanac for advice on the weather, health, cooking, or when to plant winter peas. Older people will tell you that almanacs were once so popular that they hung with a string through a hole in their cover at a handy spot for an entire year until they were replaced with a new issue—but, of course, no longer is that the case.

This country's enduring romance with almanacs has spanned over 350 years. For decades, as many as 7,000 different almanacs were consumed and saved by Americans, mainly on the basis of information. Today they are collected by generations far removed from their glory days for their design, sponsor, and content.

Most accounts say the first almanac printed in this country was published by William Pierce Mariner in 1639. Scores of similar publications followed, offering general information and even astrological and weather data for a particular year. *America's Messenger Almanac* was printed and sold by William Bradford in 1685 in Philadelphia. Early almanacs provided a listing of moon phases for planting and harvesting crops, gave social advice, and became one of the few sources of reference on home health care. The *Boston Almanac* of 1692 carried an announcement for some form of super tonic said to cure any number of things, including "distemper of the dry bell ach...." Other equally questionable tonic cures were also noted in the *New-England Almanack* of 1696. So we see that the potential for product promotion (i.e. advertising) was present even in the very early days of the almanac.

Advertising almanac, 1935, Dr. Morse's Indian Root Pills.

After a stay in prison for his publishing activities in Boston, James Franklin took his operation to Newport, Rhode Island, where he published *Franklin's Rhode-Island Almanack*, starting with the year 1728. His earthy

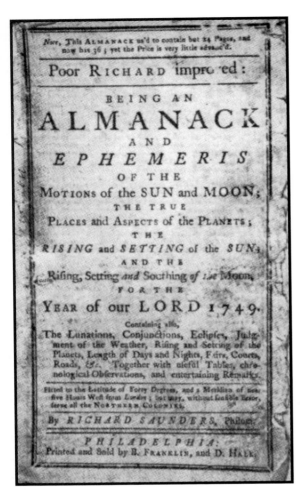

Poor Richard's Almanack for 1749, B. Franklin and D. Hall, Philadelphia. (Skinner's Inc. auction photo)

booklet pitched such sayings as "more religion than honesty," and "If you cannot bite, never show your teeth." Those almanacs with the Franklin connection are understandably quite collectible today. Other publications of that grand era included *Bowen's New-England Diary*, *Poor Job's Almanac*, *Bickerstaff's Boston Almanac*, and Ben Franklin's fabled *Poor Richard's Almanack*. Franklin used the pseudonym of Richard Sanders in those times, and thus the now-famous title of Poor Richard. From 1733 to 1748, *Poor Richard's Almanack* was published by Franklin directly, and bore the imprint "B. Franklin." After 1748, the imprint was "B. Franklin and D. Hall," as a partnership was formed. Still later issues of *Poor Richard's Almanack* were identified as from Hall and Sellers.

In the book *Treasure At Home*, author John Mebane recounts the story of how one of Franklin's almanacs "forecast the death of one Titan Leeds, his foremost competitor in the publishing field. Leeds issued a vigorous denial which received widespread publicity, thus assuring the success of Franklin's venture in the areas. His almanac became one of the earliest best sellers in America." Almanacs flourished in the second half of the eighteenth century as well, gaining true grace in New England with the likes of the *Astronomical Diary* in New Hampshire, and the *Wilmington Almanack* in Delaware.

In 1762, James Adams established the *Wilmington Almanack* after spending seven years with Franklin and business partner D. Hall. In the first issue, Thomas Fox (a character probably as fictional as Richard Sanders) gave readers this explanation of the almanac:

"Kind Reader,

Having for some Years observed those Almanacks published in America; and having formerly, in Europe, learned the Use of Mr. Thomas Street's Tables, with some others, and being willing to crowd in among the rest, I have calculated an Almanack for the Year 1762 . . ."

Interestingly, the almanac that year ended with some specific advertisements from the printer:

"Bibles, Testaments, Psalters, Spelling-Books, Primers, Merchants blank Books,

Jayne's Almanac, 1940, Dr. Jayne & Son Inc.

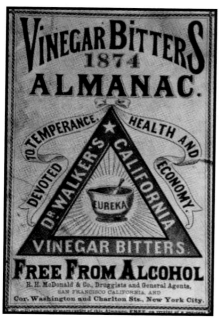

Writing-Paper, Ink, all Sorts of Blanks, Bills of Lading, Kerry Bills, Penal Bills, Bills of Sale, Arbitration Bonds, Apprentics Indentures, Bonds with and without Judgement to be sold at the Printing-Office in Wilmington. Also, very good Lampblack....Ready money for clean Linen Rags, at the above Office."

Toward the end of the eighteenth century, almanacs were appearing more and more often, almost in any city of any size that was served by an ambitious printer. In Connecticut, for example, there were almanacs published in at least three different cities between 1783 and 1800—Norwich, New London, and Hartford.

Vinegar Bitters Almanac from Dr. Walker in 1874.

Meanwhile, in Philadelphia, *Bailey's Pocket Almanac,* printed in 1786, included maps of proposed western states including Michigania, Illinois, Assenisipia, Sylvania, and Polypotamia.

There was a flood of almanacs in America during the nineteenth century. Readers could select from such titles as the *Hard Cider and Log Cabin Almanac*, the *Rough and Ready Almanac,* the *Piratical & Tragical Almanac, The Brethern Family Almanac*, and even the *General Taylor Almanac.* Many supported political or social causes, and used their title and many pages to promote their intended goal. Still others explored the potential of advertising and began to eventually expound on various products and companies. All of these things, plus the usual basic information, made them even more indispensable to the people of the East, South, and Midwest.

Ayer's American Almanac, published in 1879 by Dr. J. C. Ayer & Co., Lowell, Mass.

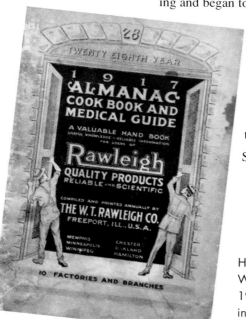

Home almanac from the W.T. Rawleigh Company in 1917, also providing cooking and medical tips.

Rawleigh's Good Health Guide, 1932.

Velvet Joe's Almanac, from Liggett & Myers Tobacco Co., 1922, Black & White.

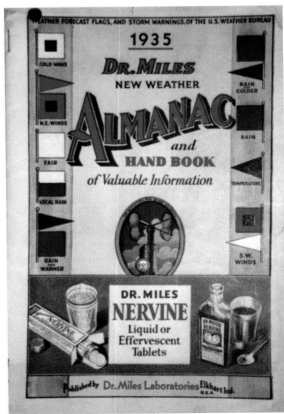

Dr. Miles New Weather Almanac, 1935.

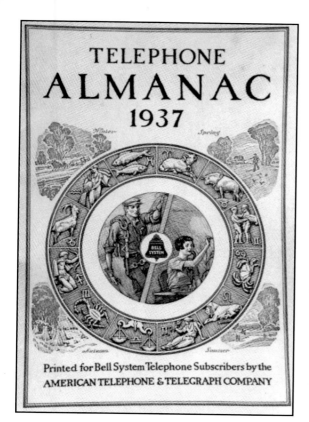

Telephone Almanac for 1937, American Telephone and Telegraph Company.

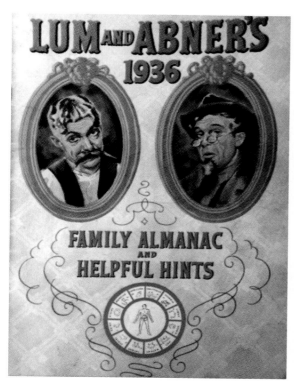

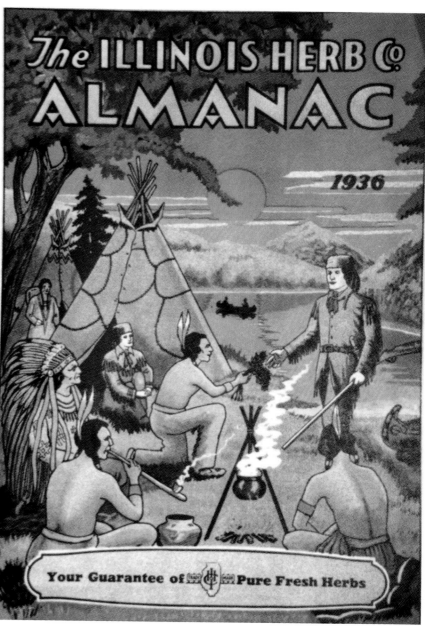

Right: Lum and Abner's 1936 *Family Almanac and Helpful Hints*, radio show premium.

Colorful cover of *Illinois Herb Company Almanac*, 1936.

DeSilver's *Almanac of 1831* listed Civil and Military officials of the United States, Masonic information, advice to mothers, and an account of "one of the most extraordinary cases ever recorded in the annals of medicine." The 1840 *American Anti-Slavery Almanac* was "calculated for New York, and adapted to the northern and middle states." Legend has it that Abraham Lincoln once used one of the then-popular almanacs to defend a man in Illinois accused of murder. Lincoln, so the story goes, showed the jury an almanac which said the "moon was riding low" on August 28, 1857; therefore, the prosecutor's claim that the defendant used the light of the moon to strike was discredited.

"Almost everyone, especially readers whose livelihood came from the sea or from farming, respected the almanacs' weather records and data," confirms the able *Family Encyclopedia of American History*. "But most of the wisdom actually centered on subjects like health, household hints, and recipes."

Watkins' Almanac and Home Doctor, 1908.

Ford Almanac for ranch and home, 1967.

The major trend for almanacs during the second half of the nineteenth century, though, was purely commercial. Some bore outlandish scientific beliefs, and offered wild medical claims. Manufacturers, especially those dealing in patent medicines, began to see the advertising potential in such "must-read" almanacs, and local merchants were encouraged to give them away to customers at little or no charge. Now, almanac choices included the likes of the *August Flower and German Syrup Almanac* from Woodbury, New Jersey, or Morse's *Indian Root Pill Almanac*. By 1890, millions of patent medicine almanacs were being distributed every year to a semi-rural populace that dearly loved them. For many families, a handed-out almanac was the only book they could afford.

Advertising played a dominant role in almanacs early into the twentieth century, as a majority were either published by those with goods or services to sell directly, or published by those with a general audience in mind and again made available through local merchants. Selections included the Rawleigh products almanacs, Watkins' *Home Doctor and Cook Book Almanac*, Studebaker's *Farmer's Almanac*, and Hill's *Southern Almanac*, distributed by the Virginia Fire and Marine Insurance Company.

Even in the 1930s and 1940s, sources for almanacs remained somewhat diverse, ranging from the F.S. Royster Guano Company and B.F. Goodrich to the folksy Lum and Abner radio show and Kellogg's *Housewife Almanac Yearbook*.

Notes to collectors:

• Very old almanacs that are historically connected, (i.e. *Poor Richard's Almanack, Rhode-Island Almanac,* the *Wilmington Almanac*) are, of course, highly prized and not likely to be found in the general marketplace.

• Almanacs that are simply very old and not connected with important historical figures or events, on the other hand, have not appreciated greatly in recent years and can still be found.

• Political and social cause almanacs, (i.e. anti-slavery, anti-Masonic) are quite collectible and have gradually increased in value in recent years.

• Almanacs with colorful and interesting (if not entirely truthful) advertising as their main thrust are still in reasonable supply, despite the fact that they were discarded annually in other times. Most are priced at less than $5 each, and will some day be looked upon as true paper treasures of the nineteenth and early twentieth centuries.

Every Day Almanac and Home Helps, 1943.

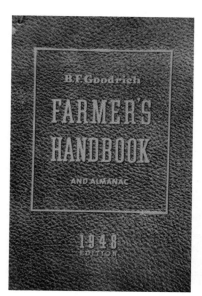

Farmer's Almanac, published by B.F. Goodrich, makers of tires and farm supplies.

The Ladies Birthday Almanac, 1967, Black-Draught.

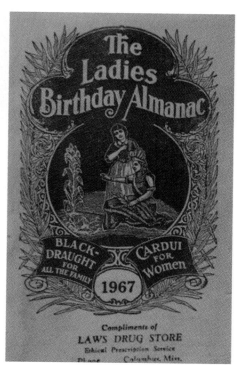

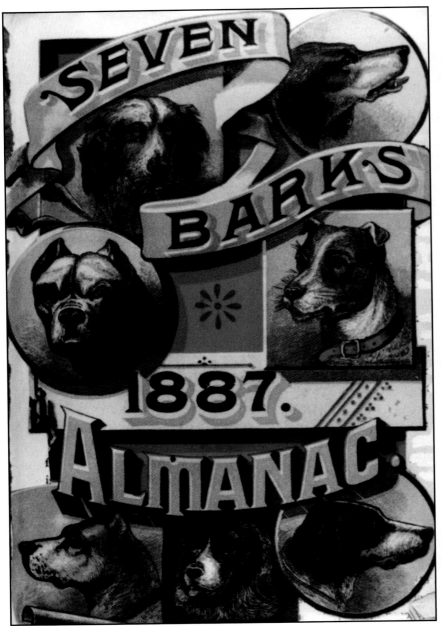

Dr. Mul-Cee's Family Practice of Medicine and Almanac, 1881.

Seven Barks Almanac, popular in the 1880s and the early twentieth century.

Right: *Dr. Jayne's Medical Almanac* and health guide from 1881. Published in Philadelphia, PA.

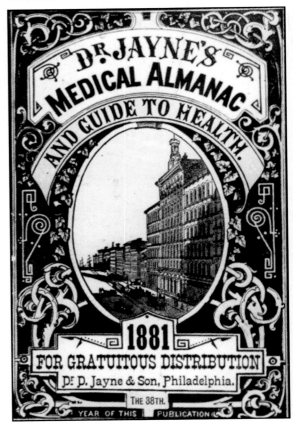

Left: *Wilson's Monarch Almanac and Guide, 1915.*

Kodol for Dyspepsia, 1908 almanac published by E.C. DeWitt & Co., color cover.

Woman at helm, cover of 1895 almanac. Warner's Safe Cure Company, 32 pages.

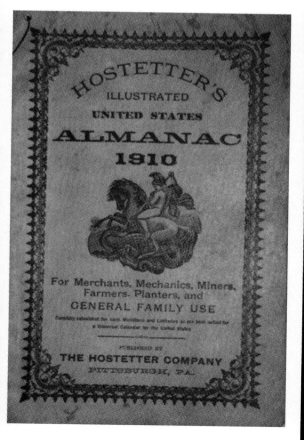

Hostetter's Illustrated United States Almanac, 1910.

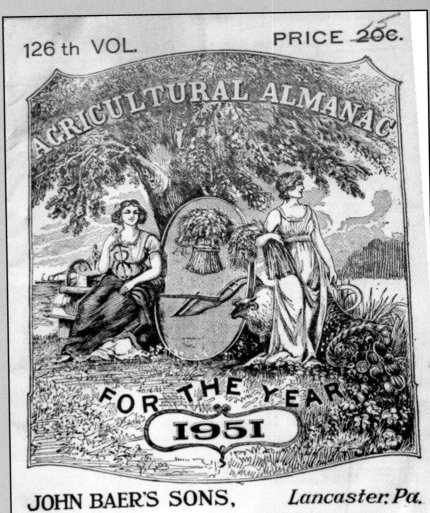

126 th VOL.   PRICE 20¢.

AGRICULTURAL ALMANAC

FOR THE YEAR 1951

JOHN BAER'S SONS,   Lancaster, Pa.

Publishing firm specialized in agricultural almanacs, 1951 issue, black and white.

Almanac for farmers, published by Royster fertilizer company, 1940, blue cover.

B.F. Goodrich *Farmer's Handbook and Almanac*, 1956.

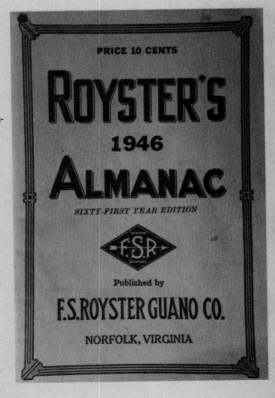

PRICE 10 CENTS

ROYSTER'S 1946 ALMANAC

SIXTY-FIRST YEAR EDITION

F.S.R.

Published by
F.S. ROYSTER GUANO CO.
NORFOLK, VIRGINIA

advertising almanac values:

1691	*H. Newman Almanac*, Boston	$35
1738	*Rhode-Island Almanack*, Stafford	$1,650
1762	*Wilmington Almanack*, Wilmington, DE	$1,200
1775	*Bickerstaff's Boston Almanack*	$280
1784	*American Independence Almanack,*	$35
1796	*New-England Almanack*, New London, CT	$48
1834	*New England Anti-Masonic Almanac*	$95
1848	*Abel New England Farmer's Almanac*	$42
1851	*Family Almanac*	$20
1860	*Tribune Almanac*, H. Greeley, New York	$20
1874	*Vinegar Bitters Almanac*, New York City	$15
1879	*Ayer's American Almanac*, Lowell, Mass.	$8
1881	*Dr. Jayne's Medical Almanac*, Philadelphia	$8
1881	*Dr. Mul-Cee's Family Practice of Medicine and Almanac*, Louisville, KY.	$10
1881	*Graefenberg Light for the World Almanac* (Graefenberg Life Preserver Pills)	$10
1887	*Seven Barks Almanac*	$6
1895	*Warner's Safe Cure Company*, woman at helm of boat,	$18
1908	*Watkins' Home Doctor, Cook Book Almanac*	$5
1910	*Hostetter's Illustrated United States Almanac*	$10
1915	*Wilson's Monarch Almanac*, Edgerton, WI	$5
1917	*Rawleigh Almanac, Cook Book and Medical Guide*, Freeport, IL	$4
1922	*Velvet Joe's Almanac and Book of Facts*	$5
1931	*Rawleigh's Good Health Guide Year Book*	$3
1935	*Dr. Miles New Weather Almanac* (Miles Laboratories) Elkhart, IN	$4
1935	*Dr. Morse's Indian Root Pills Almanac and Weather Forecaster*	$4
1936	*The Illinois Herb Company Almanac*	$4
1940	*Dr. Jayne's Almanac* (Dr. Jayne & Son Inc.)	$3
1941	*Uncle Sam's Almanac*, F.J. Haskin	$25
1942	*War Almanac* (military data), Dell Publishing	$50
1943	*The Herbalist Almanac*	$3
1943	*Every Day Almanac* (McDowell National Bank)	$3
1946	*Royster's Almanac* (F.S. Royster Guano Co.)	$3
1948	*B.F. Goodrich Farmer's Handbook & Almanac*	$3
1951	*Agricultural Almanac* (John Baer's Sons)	$4
1956	*B.F. Goodrich Farmer's Handbook & Almanac*	$3
1967	*The Ladies Birthday Almanac* (Black-Draught for all the family)	$5
1967	*The Ford Almanac for Farm, Ranch and Home*	$4

chapter four
advertising calendars

During the latter part of the nineteenth century, hundreds of commercial firms distributed calendars by the tens of thousands. It would seem logical to assume, therefore, that there would be lots of old calendars around.

Of course, that is not the case. The problem was that as the New Year rolled around, everyone was eager to replace the old calendar with a brand new one. Sure, some folks just hung the new issue over the old one for years, and others actually saved them for the "pretty picture" they bore, but generally, they were discarded. So, while initial numbers were high, and colorful images were popular, generally speaking, the survival rate of calendars was quite low.

Throughout the centuries there has been real fascination with the crafting of calendars. Historians say the remarkable Johann Gutenberg printed a calendar long before attempting his much more remembered Bible.

Prior to the 1880s, however, wall calendars for the masses were unheard of. They became popular household items when advertising became the driving force behind production and distribution.

Calendars were a natural premium for advertisers. They were relatively inexpensive when mass-produced. Major companies could have

Advertising wall calendar for Greenbrier Valley Bank, 1934, Lewisburg, West Virginia.

them printed with the latest lithographic techniques and then distributed to local merchants. Sometimes the local merchants added their own personal stamp to the calendar, and, like almanacs, any information the calendars provided was bound to remain in the home or business for the entire year.

Today, advertising calendars are still available, but in nowhere near the variety and numbers of their colorful past. Old Americans can well remember when every bank, service station, insurance company, public utility, dry cleaner, and funeral home eagerly handed them out without charge. That is hardly the case today, and a major market is the selling of an enormous selection of glossy non-advertising calendars covering every possible theme.

Complete 1954 calendar for the Pennsylvania Railroad. (Harris Auction Center photo)

Turn of the century wall calendar from Laflin and Rand Powder Company.

In the past, the dominate form of this advertising medium was the wall calendar, although pocket and desk calendars were also distributed. Wall calendars in full view of everyone for the entire year were what appealed most strongly to advertisers, and, not surprisingly, they appeal to collectors and decorators today.

When it comes to wall calendars of the past, major rank of serious collectors is comprised of those who specialize in any number of fields ranging from ammunition to World's Fairs, and from presidents to railroads. As in many other areas of paper advertising, this "crossover" factor can mean that the demand for certain types of wall calendars is quite high.

In the book *Firearms and Tackle Memorabilia*, author John Delph notes that Winchester Arms produced 100,000 wall calendars in 1896. That seems at first to be an astounding number, but considering how few apparently survived the past century, and given the growing demand from firearm buffs who now pay hundreds of dollars for an example in good condition today, the original printing apparently wasn't so great after all.

Railroad collectors tell a similar story.

"Down through the years, the railroads gave away many thousands of calendars which are now being collected," noted Stanley Baker in the fourth edition of *Railroad Collectibles*. "The rarities are the early color-lithographed

Circular calendar from 1888 for Brown's Iron Bitters tonic.

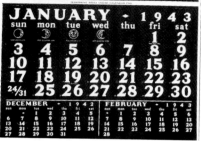

Pin-up calendar, Spirit of Liberty 1943. (Hake's Americana, York, PA)

calendars from the last quarter of the nineteenth century, which bring very high prices. Of special interest are the New York Central and Pennsylvania Railroad wall calendars which feature their famous name trains of the steam era."

Likewise, airline wall calendars from the second quarter of the twentieth century have a special following of their own. Especially sought are those from the dawn of commercial aviation's 1930s and 1940s, featuring the great airliners of the day. Other airline calendars may simply depict various tourist attractions on their routes, but still bear the names of air travel giants.

Calendars that remain from the nineteenth century typically promote standard products like Brown's Iron Bitters tonic of the 1880s. One five-and-a-half-inch circular-shaped calendar of 1888 boasted that Brown's Iron Bitters was "highly recommended for all diseases requiring a certain and efficient tonic; especially indigestion, intermittent fevers, lost of strength, lack of energy, and malaria." Moreover, this remarkable cure, according to the advertising on the back of the calendar, "does not blacken the teeth or give headache as all other Iron Medicines will." The Brown Chemical Company mailed this particular calendar to any customer for two three-cent postage stamps. The tonic itself, "unsurpassed for ladies and children," was one dollar a bottle.

The vast majority of commercial advertising calendars surviving from the twentieth century, however, are those distributed by local or regional merchants who either purchased them directly from a wholesale supplier, or who used those provided by the manufacturers of products they sold at the retail level. Examples of the latter could range from Keystone Emery Polish and Good Year Tires to national insurance companies and automobile dealerships—even calendars from the local hatchery, lumber company, or bakery are gradually becoming more and more collectible.

Swift & Company calendar, 1915, by Bessie Pease Gutman.

Good Year calendar provided by a local merchant, 1936.

Top Right: Insurance agency advertising calendar, issued in 1931.

Calendar of Lowell Fertilizer Co., 1913, wall type.

1883 Lithograph calendar.

Dr. Miles products, promoted in a 1934 advertising calendar.

Advertising calendar distributed by a local grocery store, 1925.

P.H. Mayo & Brothers Tobacco calendar, 1881, with views of crop gathering.

The artist of a particular advertising calendar can be a major factor. During the first 50 or so years of the twentieth century, a great many of the leading commercial artists, from Norman Rockwell to Maxfield Parrish, tried their hand at the financially rewarding business of doing illustrations for calendars. Today their handiwork is highly collectible, especially among those who seek out these successful artists' works in other areas. Other important artist names on early calendars (and they were usually signed) include Rolf Armstrong, George Howell Gay, Bessie Pease Gutman, Thomas Moran, Philip Goodwin, Oliver Hunt, Frederick Remington, Charles Russell, Claude Strachan, Alberto Vargas, and A.C. Wyeth, among others.

Triangular-shaped calendar, for Hood's Sarsaparilla, from 1895.

One of America's legendary calendar artists for the twentieth century was, of course, Maxfield Parrish. His annual works for General Electric Mazda Lamps became classic. In 1929, some of the sales from his distinguished prints slipped, apparently because the calendar art provided a less expensive alternative.

"People who like attractive pictures are going to cut them out and possibly frame them no matter in what form, illustrations in books, in magazines, or calendars," wrote his publisher in a letter to the artist. For collectors in this day and age, that past pre-occupation of others has seriously reduced the supply of whole, complete calendars featuring Parrish and many of the notable artists. They were simply cut-up after their particular year expired (or maybe even before) and pasted in albums, much like Victorian trade cards many generations earlier.

From the mid-1930s into the 1950s, Parrish used his talents for Brown and Bigelow, one of the nation's largest distributors of greeting cards and calendars. This agreement gave even wider distribution to Parrish calendars, which could now be available to regional and local advertisers. Prior to that time much of Parrish's calendar work was the exclusive property of Edison Mazda.

"The one thing I am really sure of is that a successful calendar picture must have strength and simplicity that catch the attention and be comprehended at a glance," wrote an executive of the firm to artist Parrish in the 1950s. "This is the one factor that is evi-

Dingel Coal Company advertising calendar from 1938.

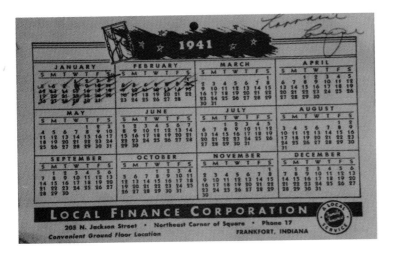

Card calendar for 1941, for a regional loan company.

dent in every successful calendar picture in our experience."

More and more today, the higher valued calendars are found fully framed at leading auctions and in larger antique malls and shops.

Specific collecting areas of advertising calendars can include particular companies, such as Atlas Tires, Campbell Soup, Coca-Cola, Firestone, Good Year, John Deere, Pennsylvania Railroad, Remington Arms, and Winchester; however, more often than not, such calendars are collected on the broader scale of soft drinks, medicine, transportation, tobacco, or farm equipment. Collectors seeking an organization may contact:

Calendar Collector Society
18222 Flower Hill Way, #299
Gaithersburg, MD 20879

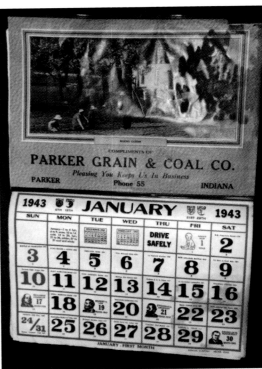

Parker Grain & Coal Co. advertising calendar from 1943.

Left: Spiceland Coal and Lumber Co. advertising calendar, 1944.

Notes to Collectors:

• Condition of any advertising calendar is important. Unmarked, without missing pages, is best. A full pad means all sheets for the various months are present.

• Celebrity advertising calendars represent a rapidly growing area of collectibility. Sports fans are wild about those that feature athletes of the past, especially baseball players. Other celebrities of the past worth looking for on surviving calendars are presidents, movie stars, military leaders, and historic figures.

• Advertising calendars are also collected by topic, (i.e. automobiles, cats, dogs, sports) as well as historical period, (i.e., nineteenth century, 1940s, 1950s).

• Like many other paper advertising collectibles, the best examples are also highly visual and frequently sought out by decorators.

Dionne Quintuplets shown on 1947 funeral home calendar.

Henry County Farm Bureau advertising calendar from 1947.

Clover Farm Stores advertising calendar from 1948.

Tydol Gasoline/Veedol Oil calendar, Dec. 1954 through Dec. 1955.
(Hake's Americana, York, PA)

Right: Regional merchant's standard issue advertising calendar, 1948.

1951 calendar for a
local dairy.

CUNA Mutual Insurance Society caricature advertising calendar distributed for 1948.

Right: Big Bear Food Stores advertising calendar from 1952.

Franklin D. Roosevelt on a 1960 auto dealership calendar.

Neighborhood Ohio bakery advertising calendar for 1955.

Fraternal wall calendar featuring art by Lawson Wood, 1960. Full color.

Sportsman's appeal on 1966 advertising calendar for lumber co.

Right: Automobile dealership advertising calendar for 1969.

1961 calendar featuring President John F. Kennedy with all the prior presidents.

calendar values

1881	Mayo & Brothers Tobacco, views of crop gathering, color illustrated, wall type	$45
1883	Compton Litho. Company, girl with bonnet, full-color wall calendar (some damage)	$25
1888	Brown's Iron Bitters tonic, circular with various Victorian figures	$45
1895	Hood's Sarsaparilla, desk calendar, triangular-shaped and illustrated	$30
1910	Laflin & Rand Powder, for firearms, wall calendar (some repair)	$585
1913	Lowell Fertilizer Co., dazzling illustration of woman and roses, full color, wall size	$225
1915	Swift & Company, artist Bessie Pease Gutman, mother and children, full color, wall size	$65
1916	Cream of Kentucky Thee Whiskey, 1915 World Series plays including Babe Ruth, full-color wall type, 34" x 26"	$4,675
1916	Dodge Publishing Co., Calendar of Cheer, cover artist Maxfield Parrish, 52-page weekly calendar	$165
1920	Max Weingarden's Cigar Store, Buffalo, New York, die-cut and embossed	$200
1921	T-R Cigars, full-color illustration of Theodore Roosevelt	$125
1923-24	Wrigley's P.K. Chewing Sweet, wall type, full-color cardboard	$15
1925	Wright Brothers grocery, summer cottage scene	$16
1928	Wright Brothers Grocery, striking color illustration of cottage, small wall type	$16
1930	Dodge Publishing Co., Calendar of Biblical Quotations, cover artist Maxfield Parrish, boxed 52-page weekly calendar	$185
1931	The Haskett Insurance Agency, children at play, color illustration, small wall size	$15
1934	Dr. Miles weather calendar, black and white, wall type	$12
1934	Greenbrier Valley Bank, full-sized wall calendar (some damage and wear)	$6
1936	Good Year and Greenfield Auto Supply, sailing ship on wall calendar, full color	$20
1936	Dingel Coal Company, scenic bridge and houses, color, wall calendar	$22
1938	Greyhound Bus Lines, scenic wall calendar, various regions of the country	$58
1940	Bicycle dealer, wall type, endorsement of bicyclists Kilian and Vopel, brands include Johnson, Iver, Columbia, Shelby, Rollfast, some creases	$40
1941	Harrisburg/Yellow Cab, wall type, child and blossoms, artist Adelaide Hiebel	$25
1941	Local Finance Corporation, card-sized calendar	$3
1941	Miles Weather Calendar, Alka-Seltzer and Nervine tables, wall type, cartoon.	$28
1941	Tydol-Veedol, paper wall type, 12 monthly pages, cowboy scene cover	$30

1943   Keystone Emery with Miss Liberty, full-sized wall calendar $35

1943   Parker Grain and Coal Company, wall calendar $18

1943   Spanky and Our Gang Safety Patrol, Gerlach-Barkow Co., color
        photo and sample calendar pad, some repair $110

1944   Spiceland Coal and Lumber Company, scenic wall
        calendar, large house $20

1945   Esquire calendar with portraits by Varga, wall type,
        12 pages complete $220

1947   George Petty calendar, wall type, one month missing, pin-up art $120

1947   Hamilton Funeral Homes, depicting Dionne Quintuplets, color illustration,
        wall type $25

1947   Henry County Farm Bureau Coop., boy and dog fishing, color illustration,
        wall type $16

1948   Clover Farm Stores, richly illustrated with mother and toddler,
        wall type $18

1948   Kendall's Kearney Hatchery, woman, baby, chicks, full-color wall
        calendar $12

1948   CUNA Mutual Insurance Society, animated characters, wall type $8

1950   Royal Crown Cola with movie star Wanda Hendrix (mint condition),
        full color, wall-sized $36

1951   Franklin Pure Milk Co., rural snow scene, color photo, wall calendar $12

1952   Big Bear Food Stores, camping scene of three bears, full color,
        wall type $18

1954   Boy Scouts of America with Norman Rockwell print, wall type,
        without tablet pages $32

1954   Gulf Farm, wall type, farm scene and school bus, 12 monthly pages,
        artist Lloyd R. Jones $22

1954   Pennsylvania Railroad, trains and skyline, full color, wall size $32

1954   Tydol and Ben Ott's Motors Inc., service station desk calendar $12

1955   Wagner's Bakery, strawberry custard pie, kitchen wall calendar $10

1960   fraternal organization with art by Lawson Wood, wall type, 12 months,
        all color $18

1960   President Franklin Roosevelt, Alexander Chevrolet Inc.,
        black and white, wall calendar $22

1961   President John Kennedy, Cash Loans Inc., full-color photo of Kennedy
        and other presidents, wall type $30

1966   Tweedy Lumber Co., full-color fishing scene, wall calendar $12

1967   Playboy's Playmate, glossy paper, 12 months, excellent condition $82

1969   Ralph Hocket auto sales, color illustration of dogs, wall type $5

1978   Ronald McDonald Play-Time Coloring Calendar, full-color cover,
        monthly pages to be colored $6

chapter five
advertising catalogs

In all the world of paper advertising, catalogs may well hold the greatest potential for the American collector. Not everyone is yet searching for them, thus a good hunt can often turn up lasting treasures.

Let me give you a true example. While researching this book, I stopped by one of my favorite antique malls just a short distance from home. I was really looking for paper advertising materials for illustrations, so I really didn't mind carefully pawing through a large box of old paper. It all appeared to have come from the same place—an old closet or attic, and I got the feeling the contents had certainly not impressed the current dealer.

After half an hour or so, I was rewarded with a small stack of almanacs and specialized catalogs. They had been generally priced (probably rather hurriedly) at $1 to $2 each. What really added to my pulse rate was the *Illustrated Manual of Tricks and Novelties,* from the Eureka Trick and Novelty Company. It was obviously old, still intact, and worth the marked price of a dollar since the topic of magic—much less documentation from a provider of magic supplies—is nearly a surefire item in the collecting world.

Further study at home made me even happier. The catalog was dated 1877, and aside from the fact that its edges had been mouse lunch at some point in the last 120 years or so, it was in pretty good shape. All pages were present, clear, and readable. My mouse friend had apparently not been hungry enough to do more than munch the outside trim. There was more good news from my own research: A nearly exact copy of this great old magic supply catalog had sold at auction a few years ago for $250. Now, allowing for the mouse-lunch factor, and allowing that it was not being sold in a major auction house, it was still worth more than $100. Who says there are not bargains to be found out there in the antique marketplace?

Eureka Trick and Novelty Company's *Illustrated Manual* and catalog, 1877.

Crepe decoration handbook and catalog, 1920 revised edition, Dennison Company.

Early advertising catalogs performed a great service to customers around the country. They provided an orderly selection of goods and services all but unknown to shoppers before. Other than the Bible, the catalog was often the only full-sized book in the American home. Certainly it was the only other book the entire family would have read. One historical text remarked that, at the turn of the century, the family Bible was kept in the living room or parlor, while the catalog was kept in the kitchen where the family spent most of their time.

"The mail order catalog has been perhaps the greatest single influence in increasing the standard of American middle-class living," noted the Grolier Society in 1947 in their volume, *One Hundred Influential American Books*. Today, those remarkable past commercial efforts of manufacturers, wholesalers, and retailers remain where they first appeared, in very collectible catalogs. Often, the products and services so carefully illustrated and priced decades ago provide amazing insight into that past for those who acquire them today.

Historians say Ben Franklin printed a small catalog for the cast-iron fireplace stove in 1744. The brochure-like booklet included one page of engraved illustrations depicting such stoves. Pennsylvania clock maker Jacob Gorgas produced an eight-page brochure catalog in 1765, complete with figures, designs, and scenes which would be engraved on watch and clock faces. Still—as was pointed out in chapter one—the majority of merchants, craftsmen, and importers of the latter eighteenth century relied on newspaper advertising and broadsides for commercial promotion. A few issued circulars of various sorts, or just listed their goods on handbills. Still others used telephone-type directories like the *American Advertising Directory for Manufacturers and Dealers in American Goods. The American Advertising Directory* was published by J. Darling and Company early in the eighteenth century, and sometimes carried the ad text and illustrations which also appeared in colonial newspapers.

During the first half of the nineteenth century, improvements in printing allowed tradesmen greater and more economical use of catalogs. By the 1850s, the mail order business, in general, and catalogs of merchandise, in particular, were in full operation. Subjects typically covered at the time included china, clocks, pottery, glassware, pewter, stoneware, and furniture. The rapid industrial expansion following the Civil War, the reasonable rates of the United States Post Office, and the country's ever-westward growth, further enhanced the use of catalogs probably tenfold in the last few decades of the nineteenth century.

"You could send the catalogs by mail even if your goods had to go by canal boat, coastal schooner, steamship, or railroad," wrote Morgan Towne in *Treasures in Truck and*

Trash. "The customer response to an illustrated catalog was immediate and gratifying."

Titles like the *Catalogue of Plumbers' Tools*, the *Illustrated Catalog of Assembly Chairs and Settees*, and *Wine Stands, Candlesticks, and Lamps* became more and more a part of a marketplace that existed in American households. Some titles could be so grand as to somewhat mislead. *The Practical Dog Book for Both the Professional and Amateur Fancier,* issued in 1884, was simply a catalog with prices for dogs and dog grooming supplies.

That same year, in New York City, James Graham began offering what he termed "antiques" through an ad on the back cover of an existing catalog. "I am constantly receiving from Europe all kinds of Rare Antiques in Furniture," noted the ad which depicted Hepplewhite furniture, Queen Anne chairs, and Sevres and Dresden china.

At that point in the 1880s, there were generally three basic groups of catalogs gradually becoming known and accepted in the growing national marketplace:

• One group were those produced directly by manufacturers, which primarily went to distributors and major industrial users. For example, the E.W. Bliss *Catalog of Industrial Machinery*.

• A second group were wholesale catalogs issued by jobbers or "middlemen" and distributors that went directly to the Main Street merchants such as operators of hardware and grocery stores. Typical was the Clifford Perfume Company's *Wholesale Barber's Supply* catalog.

• A third type, the most popular by far, were the retail catalogs made famous by Montgomery Ward, and Sears and Roebuck. Also in this popular group were nearly all major department stores of the late nineteenth century, which for a time issued their own retail catalogs. These finely illustrated catalogs encouraged the customer to shop by mail order, or in some cases, at the specially designated in-store counter.

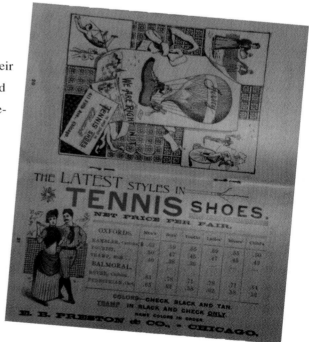

An icon of the latter group was Aaron Montgomery Ward, who lost much of his life savings in the Great Chicago Fire of 1871. A few years later he issued a 72-page catalog with illustrations, and by 1875 the Montgomery Ward company was occupying the entire floor over a livery stable and had issued a catalog of 2,000 items, including ladies hats, notions, boots, and shoes "at wholesale prices." In his early publications, Ward promoted the idea that his was "a house to sell directly to the consumer and save them the profit of the middleman." Not surprisingly, a good many local shopkeepers saw the plan as a threat to their own Main Street business. By the 1880s, many shop owners were offering customers merchandise for bringing in large numbers of mail order catalogs so they could be destroyed.

Tennis shoe styles from E. B. Preston in *Golden Rule* advertising catalog, 1890s.

Undaunted, Ward's wish books promised "satisfaction or your money back." The former dry goods salesman urged customers to pool their orders in order to qualify for a lower railroad express freight rare on shipments weighing 100 pounds or more. Meanwhile, Richard Sears had begun his own business in the 1880s with a package of watches in North Redwood, Minnesota. Within six months he had made $5,000, quit his railroad agent job, and moved to Chicago. He soon teamed up with Alvah Curtis Roebuck to eventually launch still another massive mail order business in the heart of America.

Toward the end of the 1880s, craft and art supply catalogs were becoming available, covering such areas as china painting, lithographs, picture frames, stenciling, wood burning, brass embossing, hair weaving, and shellcraft. The E.C. Allen Company had been selling household necessities and novelties by mail on a large scale for years. Likewise, two sporting goods dealers had long since mastered the lure of these publications. The Orvis Company of Vermont, and Laacke and Joys of Wisconsin, had both spent many years providing catalogs to special customers.

W. D. Leroy catalog of magical tricks and materials, ca. 1915.

By the 1890s, both Spiegel and Macy's of New York had joined the crowd of general merchandise catalog publishers. In Chicago, Sears was offering everything from a 27-piece silverware set for $5.65 to a nickel-plated revolver for $5.50. Not to be outdone, Sears and Roebuck arrived in the twentieth century with a bang. Shortly after the turn of the century, they were sending out both a Spring and a Fall catalog to a majority of American households everywhere. In 1904, they had a circulation of over one million.

Not content with general merchandise, Sears and others also began offering specialty catalogs on such topics as books and stationery, bicycles, wallpaper, locks and safes, cameras and photography, lighting fixtures, lamps, furniture, and rugs. These were produced in smaller numbers than the general merchandise catalogs, and they are generally more collectible today.

Overall, the dawn of the twentieth century saw a great expansion of the use of the catalog in the ever-growing American market-

Martinka & Company catalog of 1898 for magical supplies, New York City.

Colorful Lionel Train catalog from 1952.

Chicago Millwork Supply Co. advertising catalog from 1913.

How to Make Crepe Paper Costumes and catalog, 1925. Dennison Manufacturing Co.

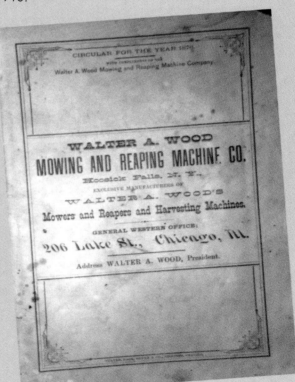

Walter Wood Mowing and Reaping Machine Co. catalog for year the 1876.

Left: *Illustrated Catalogue of Cultivator Teeth*, from J.S. & M. Peckham, 1878.

Rudge Bicycles and Tricycles catalog, 1886.

William Donaldson & Co. artist supplies and picture frames, from 1885.

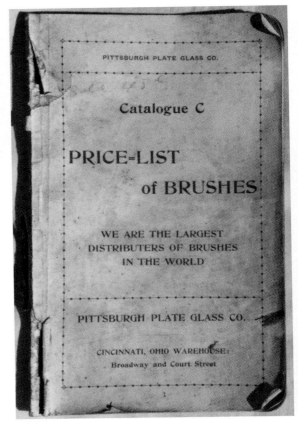

Right: *Price-List of Brushes,* from Pittsburgh Plate Glass Co., ca. 1880s, illustrated.

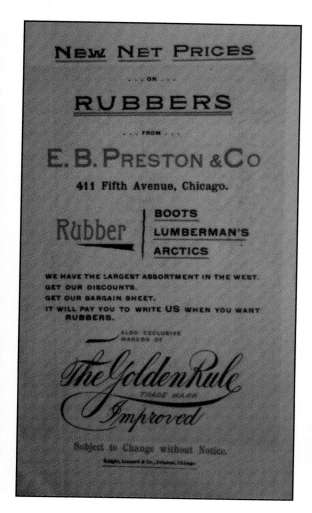

The Golden Rule catalog for rubbers and tennis shoes, 1896, from Chicago.

L.C. Smith Guns catalog from the early twentieth century.

place at all levels. Customers could page through everything from the *Abercrombie & Fitch Fishing and Hunting* catalog to Young and Town Manufacturing Company's *Locks and Hardware*. A great many of the so-called specialized titles are quite collectible today, including those dealing with clocks, glassware, pottery, furniture, toys, tools, firearms, and sporting goods. Also growing in favor are catalogs of companies which provided supplies for a fairly narrow field such as Boy Scouts, automobiles, model railroad equipment, or holiday decorations. Finally, there are the super-special areas, such as magic, which have long attracted collectors within that profession. Highly prized in that "circle" of magic are the Thayer Magic Manufacturing Company catalogs from the 1920s to the 1940s, Martinka & Company, Mysto Company, and Petrie-Lewis Manufacturing Company, among others.

Ironically, despite the vastness and abundance of advertising catalogs over the past 100 years or so, not all that many were purposefully saved. They were, of course, made to be discarded as levels of supplies and production changed from one year to another, or even from one season to the next. Not infrequently, readers were advised to destroy previous issues of a particular company's catalogs to avoid confusion over prices or available stock.

Among those catalogs that have somehow survived, many were subject to being disassembled for their enchanting illustrations. "Picture framers, interior decorators and antique dealers often break up these wonderfully illustrated old volumes for resale to institutions and collectors," noted Ron Barlow and Ray Reynolds in *The Insider's Guide to Old Books, Magazines, Newspapers and Trade Catalogs.*

Notes to Collectors:

• Advertising catalogs often have strong "crossover" collector appeal. That means the serious toy collector, firearms expert, and farm historian will be as interested in related catalogs, if not more so, than the paper advertising collector.

• No one is ready to say for sure just how old an advertising catalog must be to rightfully be collectible. Barlow and Reynolds say the most significant demand centers on catalogs from the 1930s and before; "however, most catalogs of a decade or so ago are growing collecting with the aging population."

• Such advertising catalogs are now recognized as prime research tools for any specialized category of collecting. It would be hard to argue with the *Chicago Millwork Supply*

Sears and Roebuck Grocery List catalog from January 1911.

Catalog of August Roterberg, noted Chicago magic dealer, ca. 1911.

Gurney Seed & Nursery Company catalog, 1919, from Yankton, South Dakota.

Left: Fashions of the 1920s in Mendoza Beaver fur catalog.

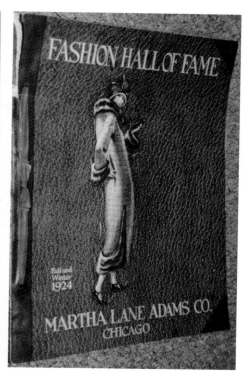

Martha Lane Adams Company fashion catalog, Chicago, 1924.

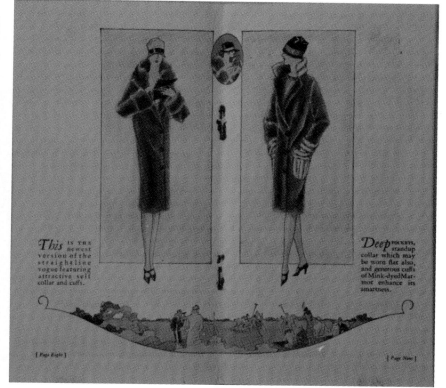

Mendoza Beaver styles in 1926 advertising catalog.

Left: *Catalog of Books, Helps and Supplies* from Beckley-Cardy Co., 1923-24.

Company's Building Material Catalog of 1913 for the types and prices of goods that year, or the full-color Lionel catalog of 1952 for the exact design and style of toy trains.

• Note should also be taken of the very specialized and sometimes striking catalogs published by the Dennison Manufacturing Company. Basically, they offered paper goods for holiday decoration and costumes during the first half of the twentieth century. These catalogs were so filled with information that today they are frequently mistaken for instruction booklets; however, they did serve to retail products and most are quite collectible.

• Collectors can also consider artists and celebrities. Famed American artist Norman Rockwell did covers for Montgomery Ward in 1925, and later for Sears in 1927 and 1932. Maxfield Parrish also did a number of catalog illustrations for firms ranging from Sterling Bicycles to the Ferry Seed Company. Shirley Temple modeled hats for the Sears catalogs of 1937 and 1938. Other stars also had roles as models for catalogs from time to time.

• Old advertising catalogs are still out there. Watch especially for those of smaller size that were published without a large number of pages. These were easily lost in stacks and bundles of other paper materials over the years, and may be well-preserved and protected from sunlight by the very paper goods that have hidden them from previous view.

Halloween Catalog, 1927, for the Dennison Manufacturing Co.

Right: Arcade Toys 1927 catalog.

Far Right: Advertising catalog for *Altman Magazine*, from 1928.

Made to Order Clothes from Sears, Roebuck, 1929.

Above Left: Summer catalog from Montgomery Ward Company, 1929.

Left: Schult travel trailer catalog, ca.1930s.

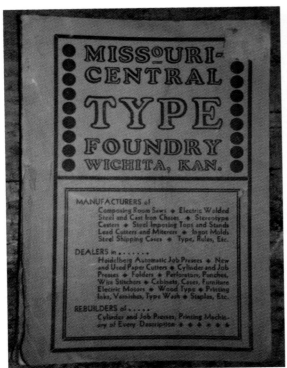

Missouri-Central Type Foundry catalog, 1933, Wichita, Kansas. 128 pages.

Right: 1934 Wards Christmas Catalog, 92 pages.

Below: 1935 LaFayette catalog sheet. Folder shows four autos built by Nash. (Hake's Americana, York, PA)

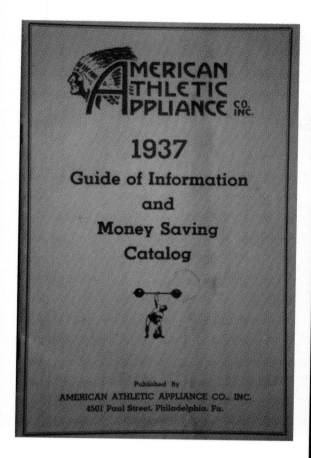

American Athletic Appliance Co. Inc. weightlifting guide and catalog from 1937.

W.S. Darley & Co. *Police Supplies* catalog, ca. 1936. Well-illustrated, 36 pages.

Promotional card for special Sears 1937 catalog.

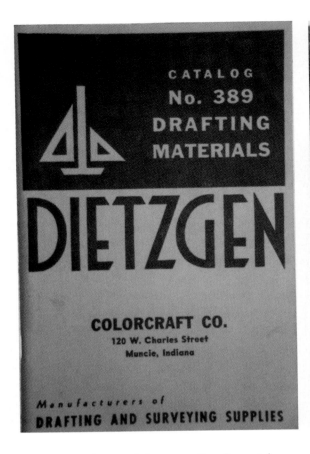

Dietzgen Drafting and Surveying Supplies catalog
from 1939.

Jim Brown's 1946 spring and summer catalog for fencing
and hardware supplies.

Left: American Field Seed Company mail order catalog, 1942-1943.

Floyd Clymer's *Catalog of Popular Motorbooks,* from 1952.

Pipe Lore advertising catalog for pipe smokers, ca. 1949.

Matchbox Collector's Catalogue, U.S.A. edition, 1968, full color.

Chevrolet catalog, 1964, full color. (Hake's Americana, York, PA)

Lane Bryant women's wear ad catalog from 1951.

Hunter, archer, gunsmith, and riflemen's supply catalog. Herter's Inc., 1957.

Summer 1954 catalog, *Master Mechanic* welding supplies company.

1875-76	Montgomery Ward and Company general catalog	$305
1876	Walter Wood Mowing and Reaping Machine Co., illustrated	$60
1877	Eureka Trick and Novelty Company's illustrated manual and catalog (chewed edges)	$105
1878	Illustrated Catalogue of Cultivator Teeth, J.S. & M. Peckham	$35
1880s	Price List of Brushes, Pittsburgh Plate Glass Co, illustrated	$20
1885	Wm. Donaldson and Company, artist supplies, picture frames	$35
1886	Rudge Bicycles and Tricycles catalog, Studdard Lovering Company	$45
1896	The Golden Rule catalog for rubbers and tennis shoes, E. B. Preston Co	$20
1901-03	Bastian Brothers flag pins, emblems, medals	$25
1905	Tribune Bicycles, Pope Manufacturing Company	$85
1907	Wm. Lehmberg Co., Lodge Costumes For All Societies, 24 pages, folded	$35
1911	Inter-State Automobile catalog, bulldog logo	$100
1911	Sears and Roebuck Grocery List catalog, January issue	$15
1913	Chicago Millwork Supply Company catalog	$38
Early 1900s	L.C. Smith Guns, Hunter Arms Company, Folton, New York	$85
1920	Art & Decoration In Crepe and Tissue Paper, revised edition, Dennison Manufacturing Company	$25
1923-24	Catalog of Books, Helps and Supplies—Beckley-Cardy Company	$35
1925	How to Make Crepe Paper Costumes, 36 pages, Dennison Manufacturing Company	$30
1926-27	Mendoza Beaver catalog, fur fashion	$25
1927	Dennison Goods for Halloween, Harvest and Thanksgiving	$36
1927	Arcade Toys catalog	$120
1928	Meco Motorcycle Supplies, illustrated	$60
1928	Gift Ideas catalog, Altman Magazine	$28
1929	Made to Order Clothes, Sears, Roebuck and Company	$30
1929	Summer catalog, Montgomery Ward and Company	$35
1934	Ward's Christmas catalog	$75
1935	LaFayette automobile catalog, Nash Built	$60
1936	W.S. Darley & Company police supplies, illustrated	$95
1937	American Athletic Appliance Company catalog, weightlifting equipment	$35
1939	Dietzgen Drafting and Surveying Supplies catalog	$25
1942-43	American's Economy Seed Special catalog, American Field Seed Company	$10
1943	Burgess Seed and Plant Company, "Food Will Win the War"	$50
1946	Jim Brown's spring and summer catalog, fencing and hardware	$18
1949	Pipe Lore catalog, smoking pipes	$8
1950	Fisher-Price dealer's catalog, 16 glossy pages, color illustrations, fine	$120

1951	Lane Bryant spring and summer sale catalog, women's fashions $12

1951   Lane Bryant spring and summer sale catalog, women's fashions $12

1951   Harley-Davidson motorcycle catalog, 16 pages, ten models,
very clean $80

1952   Floyd Clymer's catalog of popular Motorbooks $12

1952   Lionel toy train catalog, color illustrated $25

1954   Master Mechanic summer catalog, welding supplies $12

1954   Billy and Ruth Catalog, toys, color photos $55

1955   Adventures of Pinky Lee, Tiny Tears and Sweet Sue catalog,
American Character Doll Company $25

1961   Official Boy Scout Uniforms and Equipment catalog,
24 pages, clean $28

1962   Western Auto, the Family Store, Christmas catalog, 56 pages,
full color with toy section. $55

1963   Sears Christmas catalog, includes toys $75

1964   Chevrolet automobile catalog, full color $25

1966   F.A.O. Schwartz Children's World Christmas catalog, all toys $75

1968   Matchbox Collector's Catalogue, USA edition $9

1975   Super Hero Merchandise Catalogue, comic book style. Super
Hero Enterprises $25

1997   Halloween Outlet, glossy, 128 pages $5

chapter six
advertising fans

Hand fans provided, to pardon the pun, some really cool messages during warm weather for nearly a century. In fact, had it not been for central air conditioning, we might still be reading about 20 Mule Team Borax, Royal Cola, and the Wyatt Memorial Mortuary on hot and humid days.

Advertising fans promoted everything from baked goods to presidential candidates. In their time, they were inexpensive enough to allow a bridge from national to regional and local advertising. While some of America's leading manufacturers were known to use them, they could, on occasion, be found as a giveaway premium at the corner grocery store, as well. Ad fans saw service at baseball games, conventions, churches, funeral homes, and even world's fairs. They were given away in shoe stores, gas stations, hotels, and at tourist sites. At times, they were given away to travelers on trains and even airplanes.

Today, many of these advertising fans of the past are significant collectibles, and some qualify as serious antiques.

The majority of advertising fans were simple devices of paper or cardboard with a length of wooden handle in the middle. Other fans provided a simple thumb-hole instead of a handle, and still later examples just "fanned" out for hand holding. On the front was a colorful scene or product, and on the reverse was a national or local advertising message. In some cases, national and local messages were combined, as neighborhood merchants added their stamped location to fans bearing the image of a national product. Some ad fans were made with metal fasteners so they could be folded and carried in a purse or jacket for use at various times and locations. Others, like those the funeral homes provided for the neighborhood church pews, were in a fixed position and were meant to be returned after use.

Twenty Mule Team Borax advertising fan from the early 1900s.

Selection of folding advertising fans from the 1940s.

Decorated fans were, of course, popular in America long before anyone thought to put advertising on them. In that sense, they were like T-shirts and sweatshirts which, believe it or not, also once flourished without the benefit of advertising logos of any type.

As early as 1774, John and Hamilton Stevenson advertised, "Painting on silk, satin, etc. Fan Painting," in the *American General Gazette*. In 1782, a Boston painter advertised in the newspaper, "Coat of Arms and fans painted;" however, true advertising fans were generally not seen until the 1876 Centennial Exposition in Philadelphia. During the Centennial, a souvenir fan bearing pictures of the exposition's great buildings was sold to the public. At the same time, a Philadelphia store, Wanamaker's, distributed a lithographed folding fan advertising their store. Wanamaker's advertising fan offered scenes of the store surrounded by green and white floral decorations.

During the early 1880s, advertising fans were distributed to promote New York's Manhattan Market, and the William Hills Company of New York. By 1886, the business of using fans to advertise a product or place of business was depicted in a cartoon in the nationally read *Judge Magazine*. One year later, the Great Atlantic and Pacific Tea Company issued a series of advertising fans mainly featuring children and animals, with titles like "Pet of the Yacht," "Dress Parade," and "Shady Nook by the River."

Religious theme featured on fan from McBane Burial Vaults, 1949.

In the 1890s, the fledgling Coca-Cola Company decided to go with advertising fans with ambitious slogans like, "Ask at the soda fountain for a glass of cool and refreshing Coca-Cola." Even in those early days, according to Randy Schaefer and Bill Bateman, authors of the delightful book *Coca-Cola*, "Coke executives clearly understood the connection between advertising and sales."

Early twentieth-century advertising fan from the town florist.

Round-shaped Johnston's Paint advertising fan.

Right: Rublefoam for the Teeth advertising fan for E.W. Hoyt Company.

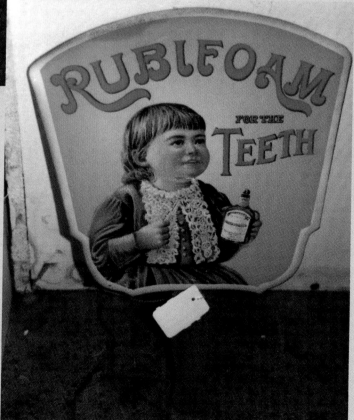

The value of the ad fans was clear. According to the authors, "as an individual was suffering from the heat of a long, hot summer, what better time to remind him or her of the cooling effects of an ice-cold glass or bottle of Coca-Cola?"

By the end of the nineteenth century, many other companies had climbed aboard the ad fan bandwagon as well. Among them were New York's Cafe Martin, Bissell's Carpet Sweeper, the Northern Pacific Railroad, Singer Sewing Machine, Tip-Top Bread, Vallejo Fine Footwear, the Waldorf-Astoria, and the great Ziegfield Midnight Frolic. Some historians think the zenith of the fan advertising fad may have been reached between the late 1800s and the early 1900s.

Man with advertising fan, full cardboard Coca-Cola Display figure, ca. 1910.

At any rate, by the early twentieth century, advertising fans were firmly established in the American marketplace. In busy New York City, the R.H. Macy Company distributed a fan with pictures of their stores. Many other commercial outlets in the Big Apple got the same idea—including Bloomingdale's and several other of the larger department stores. The message around 1900 on a fan from the Siegal Cooper Company was, "Meet me at the Fountain, The Coolest Spot in New York."

Of course, fans provided a popular ad medium beyond New York. Hires Root Beer made use of various advertising fans, and in 1904 Gold Dust and Fairy Soap issued a round cardboard fan featuring the legendary Gold Dust twins as they viewed scenes from the gala World's Fair in St. Louis.

Meanwhile, Coca-Cola continued its earlier and very successful distribution of advertising fans well into the twentieth century at record levels. "New century" thinking at the Coke company decreed that the best form of advertising came from useful items which consumers could carry around with them. Between 1906 and 1913, according to research of company records by Schaeffer and Bateman, the great company spent more for advertising fans than for Celluloid novelties, matches, pocketknives, or watch fobs. The money put into ad fans was, in fact, only second to leather good novelties during those high growth Coca-Cola boom years.

Scenic back of an advertising fan for Jordan Funeral Home, ca. 1920s.

Advertising fan for Kirk's grocery and Beatrice Meadowgold Ice Cream, ca. 1920s.

Fashionable young woman on advertising fan, ca. 1920s.
(Turner's Photo Studio.)

Firestone tires reverse, ca. 1920s advertising fan.

Hand fan from the Home Front, World War II. Ads on the back.

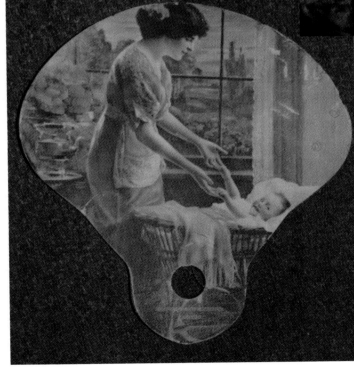

Woman and child front, Firestone tires reverse, ca. 1920s advertising fan.

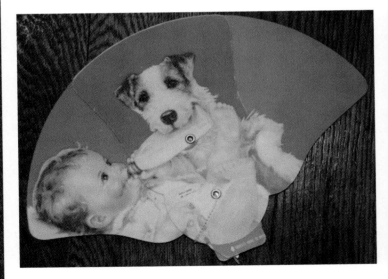

Baby with bottle and dog advertising fan, ca. 1930s. Commercial message on reverse.

At one point in 1910, Coke liked the idea of fans so much they created a large cardboard image of a well-dressed man holding a Coke advertising fan. The handy fan noted the price of Coke: five cents.

Coke, among other leading manufacturers, gave their striking fans away not only to individuals but to civic and church groups. In 1913 alone, the Coke company distributed a staggering one million advertising fans of one type or the other to groups and individuals. Schaeffer and Bateman recount that Charles Howard Chandler, the son of Coke company founder Asa Chandler, once distributed 100 boxes of rice paper advertising fans in Kansas City. According to the story, Chandler strung a quantity of them on a cord around his neck, and went floor by floor, building after building, passing them out to potential customers.

Advertising fans were also a "big hit" at baseball parks in the early 1900s. They could briefly cool the hot summer air and, just as importantly, chase away the heady cigar smoke that often filled the stands. Piedmont offered a circular fan in the shape of a large baseball on a wooden handle, urging, "get in the game and be a Piedmont fan." In New York, the Giants issued a "fan for a fan" around 1910, with various players pictured thereon. In Philadelphia, they carried a message from Eugene Mack's Base Ball Hotel. Both previous examples bore scorecards which listed the baseball players. Today, some of those ballpark advertising fans depicting early twentieth-century baseball greats are highly prized, and are regularly featured in leading sports memorabilia auctions such as those at Leland's in New York City.

By the 1920s, use of advertising fans was a regular commercial practice throughout the country. At political rallies in 1924, political crowds were given fans on behalf of presidential candidate Calvin Coolidge, declaring, "We will help to keep Cool-Idge." Elsewhere, motorists were cheerfully given giveaway fans from Skelly Gasoline, Shell Products, and others. Nationally known products advertised on fans included Moxie, Buster Brown Shoes, Emerson's Ginger-Mint Julep, Orange Crush, Tums, and Putnam Dyes and Tints.

But the appeal and the application of fan advertising was not limited to national giants. Regional and local merchants began to realize that their colorful messages could be reprinted on fans, too, and customers would keep using them throughout the summer and perhaps for other summers to come. Places like Pooler's

Advertising fan for 666 brand drugstore products, ca. 1940s.

Advertising fan for Marott's Family Shoe Store.

Advertising fan for Tokyo Crusade of World Vision, dated 1961.

Clothier Store, Reed's Women's Wear, Moe's Fresh Bakery, and St. Mary's Pharmacy offered their own ad fan, usually with a scenic view on the front.

Royal Crown had enjoined the cola battles by the 1930s with their own use of advertising fans. Among the many others joining the fan ad legions were Chevrolet, Victrola (with a die-cut design like a record), Pennsylvania Railroad, 666 Drug Store products, and Shamrock Oranges. By the 1940s, nearly every funeral home in small-town America provided religious-oriented fans with their name and three-digit telephone number on the back. These collapsing, folding fans were generously made available to patrons and churches. Another major fan category of that era included those with patriotic themes displayed in splashing color on the front—related to what would eventually be remembered as World War II. Local merchants usually purchased the fans in large numbers from a wholesaler, and imprinted their modest advertising on the reverse. Such ad fans were also frequent sights on early commercial aircraft. As many as 100 different varieties were eventually produced, ranging from Air India to a safety card widely used on DC-3 planes.

The further development and ever-wider use of central air-conditioning seriously curtailed the production of advertising fans during the 1950s and 1960s, although a few major brands remained, including Reddy Kilowatt, the utility cartoon character who promoted electrical fans.

Even in the 1960s, with such a colorful past and the end of production clearly in sight, few sources were willing to predict the collectibility of advertising fans. An exception was Katherine McClinton, prolific author of numerous volumes on antiques, including the insightful, *Complete Book of Small Antiques and Collectibles.*

Advertising fans "may be of little value today," concluded McClinton in 1965, "but the time will come when a collection of advertising fans will be of historical as well as social value. The time has already arrived when the accumulator has taken his place along with the collector as a preserver of social history and advertising Americana."

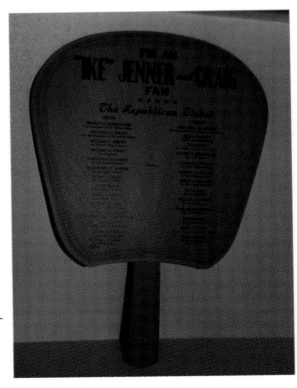

"Ike" Eisenhower and Republican ticket political fan from 1952.

Notes to Collectors:

• Like several other areas of paper advertising collectibles, generally speaking, fans with commercial messages are no longer being produced. This means the potential collector can view the entire history of such fans (roughly 75 years) in deciding ultimately which ones to collect.

• Coca-Cola fans, due to the high levels of interest in nearly all Coke collectibles, may well be cost-prohibitive for paper advertising collectors; however, for the most part, the selection of other advertising fans remains large.

• Advertising fans often project great graphics while taking up very little space—thus, they are becoming a decorative favorite for many stylish home interiors.

Milk manufacturer's advertising fan, dealer's premium, 1930s.

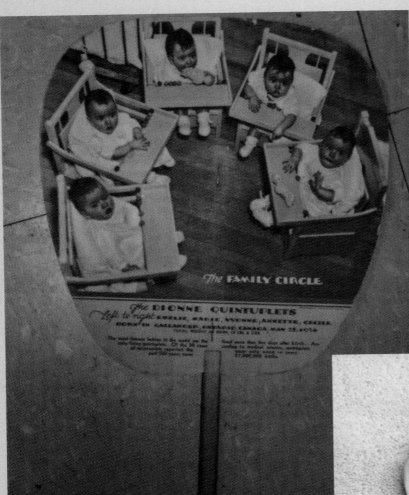

Dionne quintuplets advertising fan from Linco Gasoline, ca. 1930s.

Right: Political advertising fan featuring Alf Landon, 1936 G.O.P. presidential candidate.

advertising fan values:

America First, World War I patriotism, warships and planes, sponsors on reverse,
ca. 1917 . . . .$38

American-Maid Bread, loaf of bread pictured in full color, 1919 . . . . $58

Beatrice Meadowgold Ice Cream and Kirk's grocery, smiling child, ca. 1920s . . . $13

B.O.A.C. Airlines, Speedbird Routes Across the World, reverse airline
logo, ca. 1970s $25

Buy Defense Bonds, patriotic woman in uniform, red, white, & blue, ca. 1940s . . $35

Dempwolf's Fertilizers, full-color rooster and young lady, 1910 . . . .$50

Dionne quintuplets, ca. 1930s, from Linco Gasoline, black and white $50

Firestone Tires and Special Crown Gasoline, ca. 1920s, woman and child
on front $20

Florist, Jacob Forest, early 1900s, Greenfield, Indiana $15

Ike Eisenhower, Jenner fan, Indiana Republican fan, 1952, black and white $20

Johnston's Turkey Red Paint, round-shaped, ca. 1920s, red and white $20

Jordon Funeral Home, cottage summer scene on front, ca. 1920s, full color $6

Alf Landon, Republican presidential candidate, 1936, some wear $20

Marott's Family Shoe Store, ca. 1940s, black print $5

Milk, Cream Top bottle depicted, 1930s, dealer's premium, full color $18

McBane's Burial Vaults, 1949, front of Jesus Christ, full color $4

Ontario Drill Company, farm equipment, 1908, Baltimore, Maryland $75

Panama Canal construction, reverse Weaver Piano Company,
York, Pennsylvania, 1904 . . . .$60

Reed's Clothing and Shoes, 1930s, baby and dog on front, full color $4

Rublefoam for the Teeth, little girl with bottle, full color, E.W. Hoyt Co. $15

666 brand drugstore products, ca. 1940s, child singing with birds, multicolored . .$10

Starlight Roof/Waldorf-Astoria, patriotic woman in uniform, ca. 1940s $32

L.W. Thayer General Merchandise, smiling youngster in bow tie, reverse retail
advertising, 1908 . . . .$70

Tokyo Crusade of World Vision, dated 1961 . . . . $6

Turner's Photo Studio, fashionably dressed young woman in black, ca.1920s . . .$20

Twenty Mule Team Borax, mule head, early 1900s $50

Ward's Bread, flour mill with Dainty Maid and Tip Top brands, some repairs,
ca. 1930s $55

Wyatt Memorial Mortuary. ca. 1940s, scenic garden on front $5

chapter seven
advertising ink blotters

In terms of years, advertising ink blotters did not last all that long. While in use and circulation, and even afterwards, very few people thought they were worth saving. Now, after years of few takers, advertising ink blotters are drawing second looks from collectors.

Early in the twentieth century, nearly every product and service in America was promoted on cardboard ink blotters, which also served to absorb and help dry nasty old ink.

The range of design and printing could be simple and basic, or it could extend to something really stunning and elegant. Like their older "big sister" trade cards, any local or national business could have them printed up and distributed to customers—and, like trade cards, they could be merely black and white, or display a rainbow of bright colors.

Today, like so many other early paper advertising collectibles, they can add a spark to decorating, and they lend themselves to various themes or periods of history. Specialized collectors now seek them out for hot topics such as automobilia, Coca-Cola, footwear, motorcycles, radio premiums, sporting goods, and, of course, the leading commercial artists that created them.

In the colonial days, and up through much of the nineteenth century, writing was accomplished by dipping a basic straight pen (or quill feather) into a bottle of ink. The resulting ink image had to then be blotted, and the writing itself had to be dried. Blotting paper was well-known in America by the end of the eighteenth century. Records of the Moravian religious community of North Carolina regarding the establishment of a new paper mill contained this entry, "April 29, 1791, blotting paper will be made this week."

Denver Chemical Mfg. Co. New York, advertising blotter, ca. 1890s

Contrary to some published references, advertising blotters were actually in use in the United States as early as the 1860s. Large blotters with blotting paper on both sides were used for ledgers and hotel registers in that period, according to extensive research by Joe Nickell, author of *Pen, Ink and Evidence* (Kentucky University Press). Typically, the ledger blotters bore a significant number of newspaper-like small business service-type advertisements on both sides.

Walton shoes for girls, ink blotter, ca. 1914.

As Nickell notes, "These large blotters were intended to be used with ledgers, which could be closed upon them" once the day's entries were completed and left to fully dry.

During the early 1870s, a process was developed to allow printers to combine the blotting paper with smoother-surfaced regular paper. By the 1880s, ink blotters were being produced in smaller-than-ledger size. Advertisers no longer had to place their message directly on the "busy" ledger blotter, but could gain a much better, and uncrowded position on the smaller, improved paper. Not surprisingly then, the idea of advertising on ink blotters grew considerably.

For all the popularity of advertising ink blotters, there never was a recognized standard size. Most were small enough to be carried in a vest pocket, or mailed in a business envelope. But measurements varied considerably. Some were larger (at least longer), and others were as small as an index card.

Ink and pen users got the opportunity to clean up their act considerably with the invention of the fountain pen in 1884, by Lewis Waterman. The invention made storage of ink practical, and the constant dipping of ordinary pens became unnecessary. Still, some blotting was needed and the give-away advertising types were generally welcomed. Among the late nineteenth century blotter advertisers of note were Church & Company's Soda, Phoenix Insurance Company, Smith Brothers Cough Drops, and Chase & Sanborn Coffee.

The golden age of advertising ink blotters really dawned in the early 1900s with the commercial involvement of such now-classic companies as Arm and Hammer Baking Company, Coca-Cola, Edison's Mazda Lamps, and Pillsbury Flour. In the case of Coca-Cola, the early examples were pretty splashy for their time. Red lettering on white backgrounds boldly proclaimed the drink as one which "Restores Energy and Strengthens The Nerves."

Lion Collars men's clothing ink blotter, ca. 1915.

Dodge Brothers Trucks ink blotter and calendar from 1929, in full color.

Goodrich Hi-Press Rubber Footwear ink blotter, ca. 1920s.

Columbia Batteries ink blotter with devil and ignitor dry cell, ca. 1920s,
red and black.

Mickey Mouse featured on a Sunoco gasoline ink blotter, ca. 1940s.

By the 1920s, Coca-Cola, now a giant in the advertising medium, became exceedingly interested in attracting the youth market to their product. They appealed to youngsters somewhat indirectly through schools. Pencils, calendars, and advertising ink blotters were given to school children in vast numbers, often through the sponsorship of a local soft drink bottler. By the 1930s, the program was expanded to include Coca-Cola kits which contained writing tables, pencils, rulers, and, of course, ink blotters. Sometimes the kits cost ten cents and sometimes they were distributed free through the local school system.

Other familiar household names seen on advertising blotters of the 1920s and 1930s included Buster Brown Shoes, Bromo-Seltzer, Hygeia Coffee, Indian Motorcycles, King Arthur Flour, Maltex Breakfast Cereal, Bond Bread, Morton Salt, Pabst Blue Ribbon Beer, Pepsi-Cola, Red Goose Shoes, Reddy Kilowatt, Texaco, and many more.

Only a few advertising ink blotters were directly a part of the great voice of radio during the glory days of the 1930s and 1940s; however, some had impressive roles. One of the most well-known was that of "The Shadow," and its sponsor, Blue Coal. The coal company issued a variety of four-

B.F. Goodrich, P.F. canvas shoes ink blotter from the 1950s in red and black.

color blotters promoting their product and mentioning the radio show. Often, the blotters were subsidized by local coal distributors and included their name and business address, as well as the national advertising message.

Bond Bread, meanwhile, took a page from the Coca-Cola reader in 1938 in connection with its popular radio hero, "The Lone Ranger." On its blotters, the Lone Ranger told children, "Let Safety Be Your Rule for the honor of your School. Always be careful." A note at the bottom of the blotter said the message was prepared in the interest of safety education by the Bond Bread Bakers—certainly a noble cause.

Prudential Insurance Company also made wide use of advertising ink blotters in connection with its sponsorship of a daytime radio soap opera of the 1940s, "When A Girl Marries." Not surprisingly, their blotters featured a groom and a lovely bride. Richfield Hi-Octane Gasoline promoted both their product and the "Air Adventures of Jimmie Allen," a radio show they sponsored in 1939. The blotters colorfully depicted a bi-plane.

In the midst of the war years of the 1940s, Anheuser Busch offered a compelling advertising blotter with Uncle Sam in full color. The frankly patriotic message was to eat "plenty of bread" which, unlike many foods at the time, needed no special stamps to purchase, and was not rationed. Other featured ad blotters of the 1940s included the animated characters of Snap, Crackle, and Pop for Kellogg's Rice Krispies; Mickey Mouse joy riding for Sunoco gasoline; and J.C. Leyendecker's wonderful illustrations for American Amoco gasoline.

During the 1950s, there was a notable decline nationally in the print and distribution of ad blotters, due in part to the rise in popularity of the ball-point pen; however, old regulars like Coke, Heinz Baby Food, B.F. Goodrich, Underwood Typewriters, and others continued to make use of the medium. Additionally, thousands of different ink blotters were produced for regional and local businesses throughout the United States.

Norton Electric's football-shaped ink blotter promotes broadcasts, 1930s.

Automobile insurance ad ink blotter in three colors, ca. 1930s.

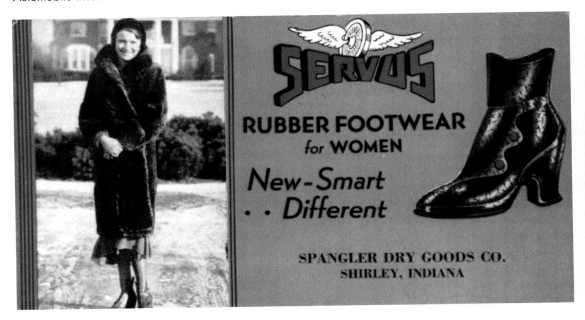

Advertising ink blotter from the 1930s promoting a national brand of women's rubber footwear.

Sunshine Cleaners advertising ink blotter from the 1930s.

Northern Pacific Railway advertising ink blotter, ca. 1930s.

American Fence and Posts, red, white, and blue advertising ink blotter, ca. 1930s.

Stark's Golden Delicious apples "actual size" ink blotter in color, ca. 1930s.

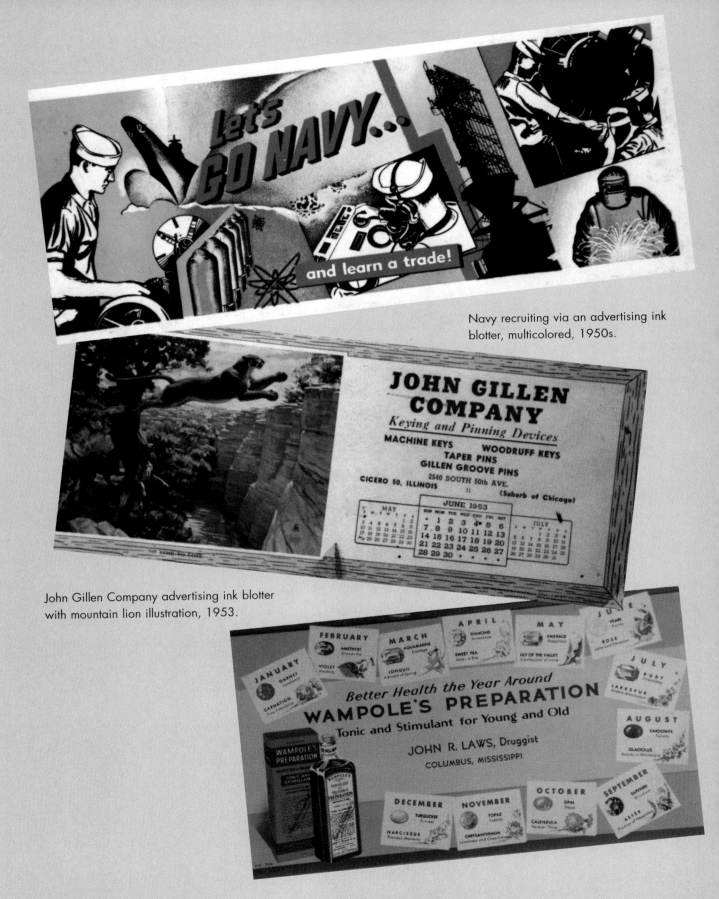

Navy recruiting via an advertising ink blotter, multicolored, 1950s.

John Gillen Company advertising ink blotter with mountain lion illustration, 1953.

Wampole's Preparation ink blotter, ca. 1930s.

By the 1960s, nearly all production of advertising ink blotters with national advertising had ended.

Some experts contend that advertising blotters will eventually take their place alongside trade cards, and move from relative abundance in the marketplace to become fairly scarce and, thus, appreciate in price. At present, a majority of ad blotters are both available and reasonably valued. The relatively few costly ones have special characters such as Disney's Mickey Mouse or the Lone Ranger. Highly collectible products, such as Coca-Cola, feature highly regarded artists such as Leyendecker or Norman Rockwell—or relate to a special theme, such as radio's "The Shadow," or World War II's patriotism.

At their zenith, ink blotters had a very important role in advertising. Their clear and direct graphics, for the most part, appealed to the public—not unlike billboards that once dotted U.S. highways. Today they are no longer a working part of the commercial community, but they undoubtedly will have an increasingly brighter future in the community of paper advertising collectibles.

Coca-Cola ink blotter in full color, 1960.

Tube-Turn welding supplies advertising ink blotter with workers, ca. 1950s.

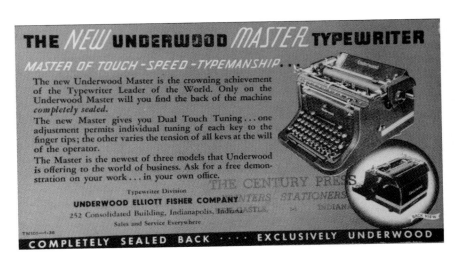

Underwood Master Typewriters ink blotter, ca. 1930s, in blue and black.

Morton Salt ink blotter, full color, ca. 1930s.

Midwest Tool & Mfg. Co. ink blotter with Lawson Wood cartoon work, August 1940.

Griffin ABC shoe polish advertising ink blotter, multicolored, ca. 1940s.

Certified Seed advertising ink blotter with female farmer, ca. 1940s.

Anaconda Sheet Copper three-color ink blotter, "There to Stay," ca. 1930s.

advertising ink blotter values:

American Fence and Posts, America's largest selling fence, red, white, and
blue, 1930s $3

American Radiator & Standard Sanitary, orange and white, 1950s $3

Anaconda Sheet Copper, gutters and drain pipes, 1930s $3

Anheuser-Busch, Uncle Sam promoting bread, 1940s $9

Anheuser-Busch, National Wartime Nutrition Program, 1940s $8

Arm & Hammer Baking Soda, ca. 1910 . . . .$4

Arm & Hammer "Old Reliable" Baking Soda, w/ 1916 monthly calendar,
some brown spotting $9

Arnett's Tire Shop, 1930s, gasoline and service station $5

Bastian Brothers Co., badge, button, emblem products illustrated,
ca. 1930s, unused $11

Bell Telephone, Don't Write—Talk, red, white, and blue, ca. 1916 . . . .$20

Big Store, retail items pictured, 1939 . . . .$3

Blue Coal Co., mentions "The Shadow" radio show, 1930s $25

Bond Bread, Corsair Navy fighter plane, ca. 1940s $15

Bond Bread, depicts Lone Ranger and safety rule for school, 1938 . . . .$22

Borden's Dairy products, Elmer the cow in Santa outfit, 'Buy Extra War Bonds,'
ca. 1940s $20

Buster Brown Shoes, for boys and girls, full color, 1930s $12

Certified Seed of Indiana, female farmer, color photo, ca. 1940s $4

Chase & Sanborn coffee, full color, stamped store name, copyright 1886,
some wear $11

Coca-Cola, Restores Energy and Strengthens Nerves, red on white, 1906 . . . . . .$120

Drink Coca-Cola, full color, unused, copyright 1951 . . . .$25

Coca-Cola, Over 60 Million A Day, unused, copyright 1960 . . . .$12

Coca-Cola, full color art, dated 1937, unused, excellent condition $52

Columbia Batteries ignitor dry cells, ca. 1920s $3

Cow Brand Baking Soda, ca. 1920s, unused $10

Davidson's of Indiana, fashion furs, 1950s $2

Denver Chemical Mfg. Co, ca. 1890s $6

Dodge Brothers Trucks, farmer's pickup, full color, 1929 . . . .$8

Edison Mazda Lamps, woman holding bulbs, full color, 1912 . . . .$12

John Gillen Company, keying and pinning devices, canyon scene, 1953 . . . .$2

B.F. Goodrich, P.F. canvas shoes, 1950s $3

Goodrich Hi-Press rubber footwear, figure and truck, multicolored, 1920s $3

Griffin ABC liquid or paste shoe polish, 1940s $2

Hardy-Burlingham Mining Company, Hard Burly Block Coal, red and
white, 1940s $3

Heinz Baby Foods, unused, full color, ca. 1950s $10

Hilberg, meat wholesaler, 1930s $2

Kellogg's Corn Flakes, full color, ca. 1940s, unused $4

Kellogg's Rice Krispies, full color Snap, Crackle, and Pop, artist Vernon Grant, ca.
1930s, unused $9

Lion Collars, men's clothing brand illustrated, ca. 1915 . . . .$3

Mazda/General Electric Co., woman holding light bulbs, art nouveau style, unused,
copyright 1912 . . . .$23

Morton's Iodized Salt, with grocery store imprint, ca. 1930s, some wear $8

Midwest Hardened & Ground Sleeves, signed artist Lawson Wood, monkey
featured, 1940 . . . .$5

Navy, Let's Go Navy, action scenes, multicolored, 1950s $3

New Castle Business College, our graduates get good positions, two
graduates, 1930s $4

Northern Pacific Railway, North Coast Limited, black and maroon, 1940s $4

Norton Electric Co., football-shaped, promotes football broadcasts on radio,
ca.1930s $5

Ohio State Life Insurance Co., fountain scene, 1920s $2

Our Gang, stars grouped with Majestic Electric Radio, browntone, ca.
1920s, unused $60

People's Bank, scene of India, 1950s $2

Pillsbury Flour, man holding flour sack, 1910 . . . .$5

Prudential Insurance, mentions "When A Girl Marries" radio show, bride and
groom, 1940s $18

Reddy Kilowatt, black, white and tan, Philadelphia Electric Co., 1939 . . . .$25

Servus, footwear for women, full-view photo of model in furs and boots,
orange, 1930s $5

Southern Marble & Stone Co., black and gray, ca. 1910 . . . .$2

Stark's Golden Delicious apples, apple pictured, 1930s $2

State Automobile Insurance Association, red, white, and blue, 1930s $3

Sunoco Nu-Blue gasoline with Mickey Mouse driving car, full color, 1940s $75

Sunshine Cleaners, woman dyeing and cleaning, blue on white, 1920s $3

Underwood Master Typewriters, two models pictured, 1930s $3

Walton Shoes, ca. 1914, depicts girl in full period dress with shoes $5

Wample's Preparation tonic, product pictured, ca. 1930s $3

chapter eight
advertising in magazines

Magazine advertisements. Once they were tossed away. Now we frame them and hang them on the wall, both in appreciation and for decoration.

There was a time long ago when magazine ads were simply considered part of the magazine, if they were considered at all. Throughout the twentieth century, they have evolved from advertising to trash, and finally advanced to a sort of collectible art work. Magazine ads are collectible in a number of ways, including by artist, celebrity, company, and product. Ads for automobiles, Coca-Cola, sports figures, and toys have long been sought, but now the field has expanded to cereal, fashion, tobacco, transportation, gasoline and service stations, and even fast food restaurants.

Certainly magazine advertisements existed long before the 1890s, but magazines were largely secondary to newspapers throughout most of the nineteenth century. By the late 1800s, major manufacturers had begun to realize the tremendous potential of advertising in general market magazines. Soon-to-be artist legends like J.C. Leyendecker and Maxfield Parrish ended up with more work than they could handle.

Readers could consider the appeal of Pear's Soap, Pillsbury's Vitos Wheat Food, Pettijohn's Breakfast Food (featuring dancing bears), or Cream of Wheat. Coca-Cola had also joined the ranks of magazine advertisers. In the midst of the boom came tobacco companies who saw the opportunity for serious campaigns for their new products.

"Fueling the national call for tobacco was advertising which literally thundered across the land in scope and breath," noted Gerald Petrone in the sweeping volume, *Tobacco Advertising: The Great Seduction*. "Attention was directed to newspapers and magazines. What had for years lain as vast, overlooked and underestimated avenues of communication had, by 1900, come to the front as a fresh, new way of merchandising a full range of goods to the nation's consumers."

Dancing bears featured in Pettijohn's Breakfast Food ad from 1899.

Woman and Pillsbury's Flour in 1890s magazine ad from *Frank Leslie's Illustrated*.

Female golfer for Pears' Soap, 1899, *Frank Leslie's Popular Monthly*.

In 1911, executives of the Campbell Soup Company had expanded their own advertising horizons to include not only their original trolley car cards, but newspapers and magazines as well, in advancing their product and their popular Campbell kids.

"In the trolley car cards we concentrate on the Kids; in newspapers, the Kids and the car; in magazines, mainly the can but without losing sight entirely of the Kids," noted Campbell spokesman Leonard Frailey at the time. "The Kids are almost able to look after themselves."

That same year, magazines indicated they, too, were able to take care of themselves in the marketplace. The Curtis Publishing Company, owners then of *Ladies' Home Journal* and *The Saturday Evening Post*, hired an expert to conduct what was later known as the Ash and Trash Survey. They directed their agent to survey 56 magazine subscribers of various backgrounds in Philadelphia. After sorting through thousands of containers, they determined that magazine advertising was highly effective, and in all households, and more to the point, the heavily advertised Campbell soup was popular with all economic classes in the survey.

The excitement generated by that survey and the tobacco industry's decision to jump unabashedly into the marketplace, helped create a boom era of magazine advertising. Between 1912 and 1920, a major marketing war broke out in national magazine advertising involving Turkish cigarettes. The result was highly colorful and attractive ads from such brands as Egyptian Deities, Fatima, Helmar, Murad, and others.

They were, of course, joined by a host of other national brands seeking to obtain a share of the consumer marketplace of magazines. They ranged from Grape-Nut Food, Studebaker automobiles, and Kiddie-Kar Scooters, to the D.M. Ferry Seed Company (Maxfield Parrish) and Arrow Shirts (J.C. Leyendecker).

For Parrish, the business of illustrating magazine advertisements had never been better. In 1915, at roughly $1,000 per job, the artist could afford to be selective. He wrote to his agent, "If you have an idea you would like worked out, say something on the same order as the Dutch Boy or the Colgate soap ad, let me know about it; I will gladly undertake it, and if I do not see a result that will do justice to myself or to you or to the product advertised, I will tell you frankly that I do not want to under take it."

Meanwhile, Leyendecker's "illustrations for Arrow Shirts and Chesterfield cigarettes were high-style realistic portraits that have come to symbolize the Deco period for the many who admire and collect them," observe Robert Heide and John Gilman in their distinguished book, *Popular Art Deco*. "Other famous illustrators like James Montgomery Flagg and Norman Rockwell represented the indomitable spirit of Americanism throughout changing times, each in his own inimitable, highly original, and easily identifiable manner. Magazine ads and prints by these artists are now avidly collected, framed, and used as nostalgic decoratives for the home."

During the Roaring Twenties, magazines prospered with a rapidly growing variety of advertisers. Parrish further used his talents to produce JELL-O's "Polly Put the Kettle On" and a number of other related works for the Genessee Food Company. Similarly, Quaker Puffed Wheat and Post Toasties extended their appeal in women's magazines; and Goodrich Tires and Texaco began reaching out for Americans who were, in turn, taking to the open road.

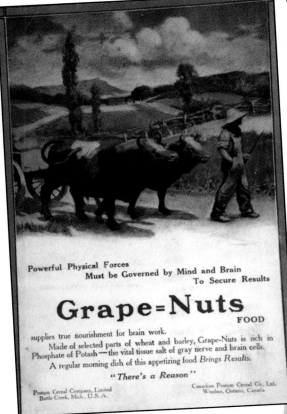

Farmer and oxen promote Grape-Nuts cereal in this full-color 1912 magazine advertisement.

Arrow Shirts advertisement of 1912, by J.C. Leyendecker.

Pedal car featured in a Texaco advertisement from 1940.

Pedal car featured in a 1940 magazine advertisement for Dole Pineapple Juice. Ad appeared in the April 1940 issue of the *American Home*.

Celebrity "Red" Hulse featured in a Camel Cigarette magazine ad from the 1940s.

Colorful Texaco magazine advertisement from the 1950s.

American Airlines magazine ad by artist Alfred Parker, from 1950.

JELL-O featured in magazine ad with The Brenstains, from 1952.

Burger King magazine ad "Home of the Whopper," 1966, full color.

Theater magazines of the 1920s captured an elite advertising audience. Dated 1923.

Lucky Strike ad from 1935 features woman in white gloves. (*Literary Digest*)

Kelly Springfield Tires magazine ad in full color, from 1923.

Advertisers also began to seek out special markets. Theater audiences in New York, Chicago, and other cities, for example, were considered not only upwardly mobile but captive—at least for the evening. Advertisers discovered they could reach these affluent readers through specially prepared publications as the audience waited for the curtain to go up. Striking color ads appearing in these special theater program publications during the 1920s and early 1930s, from Kelly Tires to Fatima Cigarettes, were some of the finest in print, and are prized today.

By the late 1920s, the ever-ambitious tobacco industry used magazine ads to directly appeal to women. Previously, women were not considered to be major customers, and it was generally not socially acceptable for them to even smoke in public. These ads served to change all that. Typically, the ads showed very attractive and sophisticated women. For a time, in anticipation of competition from candy products, cigarette advertisements boldly and flatly advised women to "Reach for a Lucky instead of a Sweet," or similar anti-candy messages.

During the 1930s, the tobacco, cereal, and soft drink companies were joined by the likes of Columbia Bicycles, the Chesapeake and Ohio Railroad, Gillette Razors, Texaco Fire Chief, Schenley Whiskey (Norman Rockwell) and countless other commercial firms seeking to reach America's ever-expanding number of reader-consumers.

Coca-Cola continued its mastery of magazine advertising in the 1940s, first with soldiers depicted at various military sites during World War II, and later with the battle-cap-wearing Sprite Boy. Coke may well have dominated that period to the point that many wonderful examples can still be uncovered today. Their ads regularly appeared in *Life, Liberty, Literary Digest, Colliers'* and *The Saturday Evening Post.* Moreover, for nearly 30 years starting before World War II, Coke also repeatedly advertised on the back covers of *National Geographic Monthly.*

Coke, in fact, built such a paper advertising empire that collecting and viewing just these examples "can be very rewarding and is like reviewing the history of America for the last 100 years through the styles and fashions, the wars, the sports and entertainment," according to Allan Petretti, author of *Petretti's Coca-Cola Collectibles,* and related books. "The best thing about collecting Coca-Cola ads is that you can create your own history book of this country without a large investment," Petretti notes.

Coca-Cola magazine ad, ca. 1942.

Magazine ad depicts Coke in Alaska during World War II. Signed by the artist.

Top: Soda fountain scene depicted in 1947 advertisement for Coca-Cola.

There's this about Coke...

"It sure is preferred"

Yes, preferred is the word
because Coke is the most
asked-for soft drink in the world.
That's because of its matchless flavor,
welcome everywhere, equalled nowhere.
And because its goodness never changes,
Coke is a life-long pleasure.
Naturally, it's preferred.

Now's the time for JELL-O

Isn't it wonderful when you can still buy the
family's favorite dessert for mere pennies? Kids
from 6 to 60 really go for a big, luscious dish of
Jell-O and it's so good for 'em, too!

JELL-O ad by Hank Ketchum, "Dennis the Menace"
illustrator; 1952, full color.

Magazine advertisement from
1954 features Coke and classic
soda fountain.

What makes a Lucky taste better?
"IT'S TOASTED"
to taste better!

LUCKIES TASTE BETTER, Cleaner, Fresher, Smoother!

Baseball great Ted Williams for Lucky
Strike, in 1954 *Collier's* magazine ad.

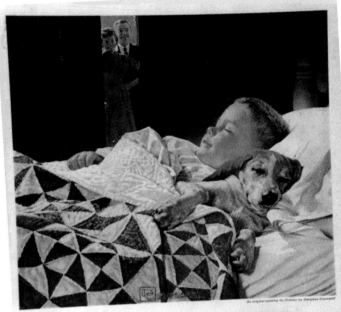

End of a frisky day...

Friskies provides up to twice the nourishment of low-quality dog foods

Some canned dog foods may fill without fully nourishing...no matter how much your dog may eat! Canned Friskies is a complete diet containing every food element dogs are known to need...up to twice as much nourishment per can as low-quality dog foods. The principal ingredient in Friskies is *real* meat, inspected and certified horse meat. Every can is prepared to the high standards of the Carnation Company and the U. S. Government.

Only a canned dog food that fully nourishes can bear this U.S. Govt. Seal

CARNATION COMPANY,

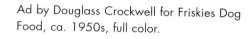

Quality at your feet...

BROWN SHOE COMPANY

Always the best buy in school shoes—perfect-fitting Buster Browns

When you buy Buster Browns you're buying more than a pair of shoes. You're buying priceless protection for your child's growing feet. Safeguarded into correct growing habits by the trusted Buster Brown 6-Point Fitting Plan. It takes more time, but it's time well spent if it gives you peace of mind. Priced according to size, 5.99 to 7.99. Higher Denver West. Buster Brown Division, Brown Shoe Company. St. Louis.

BUSTER BROWN.

MORE BOYS AND GIRLS WEAR BUSTER BROWN SHOES THAN ANY OTHER BRAND.

Buster Brown magazine ad by artist Alex Ross, from the 1950s.

Halloween pumpkin by artist Ludwig Bemelens; magazine ad from the 1950s.

smart punkin

Three-flavored fun * from Mars' sunlit kitchens—the best liked chocolate-covered candy bar in all the world...Milky Way.

* 1. Rich milk chocolate
    2. Golden caramel
    3. Creamy chocolate malted milk nougat

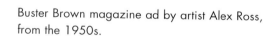

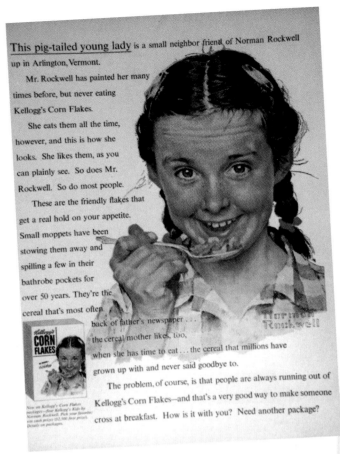

Magazine ad by Norman Rockwell for Kellogg's
Corn Flakes, 1954.

Kellogg's Rice Krispies magazine ad with Snap,
Crackle, and Pop, 1941.

Smiling Tony the Tiger in 1950s
Kellogg's Sugar Frosted Flakes
magazine ad.

Kellogg's Rice Krispies, meanwhile, went to print in the 1940s to formally present Snap, Crackle, and Pop, while still more inroads in magazine advertising were made during that era by Greyhound Bus, Radio Flyer toy wagons, Philip Morris, and Boeing Airliners, among others. Also during the 1940s, Royal Crown Cola upstaged the tobacco companies a bit with their own delightful series of full-color magazine ads using lovely Hollywood movie stars such as Shirley Temple, Dorothy Lamour, Barbara Stanwyck, Rita Hayworth, Hedy Lamarr, Lauren Bacall, and Ann Sheridan.

Candy bars offered up a big bite of the market during the 1950s with full-color magazine advertisements, particularly in the enormously popular *Life* magazine. Meanwhile, eternally talented Norman Rockwell created a delightful series of youngsters for Kellogg's Corn Flakes, including a pig-tailed young lady who was the artist's neighbor in Arlington, Vermont. For their Sugar Frosted Flakes brand, Kellogg's unveiled a smiling, unforgettable, and very animated Tony the Tiger for 1950s magazine readers.

Notable magazine advertisements which made favorable impressions during the 1960s included games from Parker Brothers, Big Mac from McDonald's, the supersonic

Light Six Studebaker, featured in 1918 magazine ad, in full color.

Cream of Wheat magazine ad from 1912 in black and white.

Left: Big Mac premier magazine ad. Full color, from McDonald's, 1968.

Bugs Bunny, featured for Brach's Easter candies; full color, 1959.

Yogi Bear stars in Kellogg's Corn Flakes magazine ad, 1961.

Renault 8 featured in a black and white magazine ad from 1966.

Classic Santa with Coke, on the back cover of a 1961 *National Geographic* magazine.

That's using your pumpkin! When the job is finally perfect—sit back, relax, refresh with an ice-cold Coke.

things go **better with Coke**

Coca-Cola ad for Halloween, ca. 1964.

things go **better with Coke**

Who ate my Post Toasties?

Trust a redhead to stand up for her rights…even in this man's world. Little sister wants Post Toasties and nothing else. They're the only corn flakes so crisp, so rich in golden-corn flavor. So, Mother, give Sis a break and hurry to the store for more. **For goodness sake**…get Post Toasties!

For your rugged little individualists… get Post Toasties in the handy new Redi-Pak! Eight separate servings…always crisp and fresh in these individually sealed boxes.

Classic Santa for Coke, by artist Haddon Sundblom, in a 1963 magazine advertisement.

Post Toasties magazine ad by artist W. Darrow Jr., ca. 1960s.

SST from Boeing, and increasingly more elaborate ad campaigns from the makers of Coke. For all of their glory, however, another national advertising medium—television—was rapidly gaining public attention, and the zenith of magazine ads had passed.

Today, from Avalon Cigarettes to Zippo lighters, nearly all collectible topics have been extended to include magazine advertisements as related printed products. Those who treasure Lionel Trains, View Masters, radios, flashlights, fountain pens, jewelry, or American-manufactured china also, understandably, desire to possess the magazine ads that once promoted these products to a curious public.

Of course, the work of highly respected commercial artists remains in demand as we near the end of the twentieth century, from Parrish and Rockwell to Lyendecker and cartoonist Hank Ketchum. A good rule of thumb is that the work of an artist, who had enough status to sign magazine ads, is well on the way to being collectible today. Moreover, some stylish magazine advertisements are collected by era and by art period, such as Art Deco, Victorian, and Modern.

Coke magazine ad from 1930 features Edgar Bergen and Charlie McCarthy.

Elegant Packard automobile ad from 1931 *Literary Digest.*

Right: Magazine ad featured Fred and Adele Astaire for Chesterfield Cigarettes, 1931.

Magazine ad by Maude Tousey Fangel, 1936 *Ladies Home Journal.*

Striking Nash automobile ad from 1940 magazine, by artist Steven Dohanos.

Notes to Collectors:

• As noted, the time of lavish magazine advertisements largely ended with the 1960s. Major national advertising revenues after that time mainly went to television.

• Experts disagree on whether an old magazine should be left intact or if, indeed, the advertisements should be "rescued" independently; however, the fact remains that, for the most part, colorful magazine advertisements that can be framed remain the more desirable of the two among collectors.

• Condition is, of course, important, but the good news is that even dog-eared old magazines with torn-off covers often still contain ads in near-mint condition.

• Unlike some paper advertising collectibles, the quest for most magazine advertisements is in the early stages. A vast majority of them can be found for well under the price of a couple of movie tickets.

For further reading:

Advertising, Confident Collector series, by Dawn Reno, Avon Books.

Huxford's Collectible Advertising, by Bob and Sharon Huxford, Collector Books.

Petretti's Soda Pop Collectibles, by Allan Petretti, Antique Trader Books.

Tobacco Advertising: The Great Seduction, by Gerald Petrone, Schiffer Publishing.

concerning magazine ad values:

American Airlines, by artist Alfred Parker, 1950, full color $4

Parker Brothers games, 1964, McCall's $5

Brach's Easter Candies with Bugs Bunny, 1959, full color $5

Burger King, Home of the Whopper, 1966, depicts new store, full color $5

Buster Brown Shoes by artist Alex Ross, 1950s, full color $5

Camel cigarettes, 1940s, with pilot/celebrity Red Hulse, full color $5

Coke with Halloween theme, 1964, man, woman, and jack o'lantern, full color . .$6

Coke with classic Santa, 1963, artist Haddon Sundblom, full color $10

Coke and Sprite Boy, 1942, full color $10

Coke with radio's Charlie McCarthy and Edgar Bergen, 1930s, full color $15

Coke with soda fountain and soda jerk, 1954, color illustration $4

Coke with crowd scene from soda fountain counter, 1947, color illustration $5

Cream of Wheat, 1912, Black Chef Rastus, black and white sketch $20

Dole Pineapple Juice, child riding pedal car, 1940, red, orange on black

   and white $6

Friskies Dog Food, ca. 1950s, sleeping youngster and dog, artist Douglas

Crockwell, full color $5

Grape-Nuts Food, farmer and oxen, 1912, full color $12

Hires Root Beer, 1915, black and white $20

JELL-O family shopping by "Dennis the Menace" artist Hank Ketchum, 1952,

   full color $5

JELL-O youngsters' Halloween party, illustrated by the Brenstains, 1952,

   full color $7

Johnnie Walker Scotch whiskey, 1966, full color $3

Kellogg's Corn Flakes with early Tony the Tiger, 1950s, full color $7

Kellogg's Corn Flakes with Yogi Bear, 1961, full color $4

Kellogg's Corn Flakes with pig-tailed girl by artist Norman Rockwell, 1954,

   full color $9

Kellogg's Rice Krispies with Snap, Crackle, and Pop in schoolroom, 1941,

   full color $5

Kelly Springfield Tires from *Studebaker Theater* magazine, 1923, full color $20

Kiddie-Kar Scooters, 1919, *Ladies' Home Journal*, full color $20

Lucky Strike cigarettes, 1954 featuring baseball legend Ted Williams,

   color photo $15

McDonald's introduces Big Mac, 1968, a meal disguised as a sandwich,

   full color $5

Nash sedan automobile, 1940, by artist Steven Dohanos, full color $8

Pear's Soap female golfer, 1899, *Leslie's Monthly*, black and white $15

Pettijohn's Breakfast Food, dancing bears, 1899, black and white $8

Pillsbury's Vitos Wheat Food, woman in kitchen 1890s, black and white $6

Post Sugar Crisp treat-pak, early 1960s, Halloween theme and costumed child . . .$5

Renault 8 automobile, 1966, black and white photo $5

Squibb's Cod Liver Oil, 1936, infants illustrated by Maude Tousey Fangel,
   browntone $10

Studebaker Light Six automobile, 1918, full color $18

Texaco, Dad's service station hat, 1950s, full color $5

Uncle Wiggily game, 1929 *Ladies' Home Journal*, black and white $22

Halloween theme magazine ad from the early
1960s; artist Dick Sargent.

Johnnie Walker scotch magazine ad from
1966, in full color.

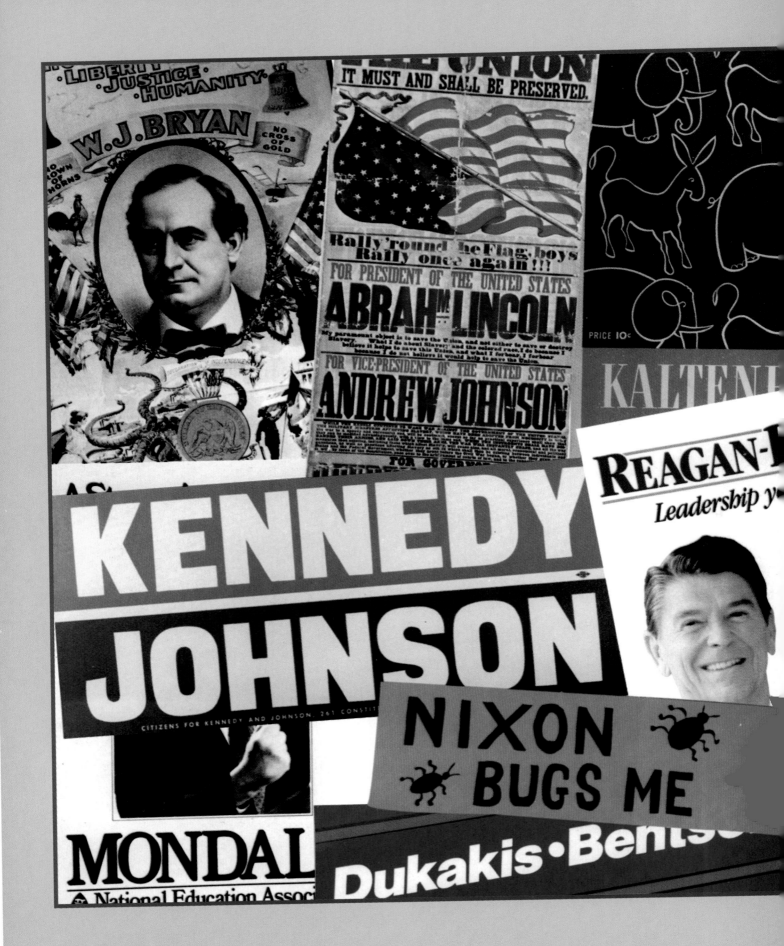

chapter nine
political advertising

"If I were you I'd up that to about 100 percent."
John Connally, presidential candidate and former governor of Texas, on learning that a congressional campaign spent 50 percent of their funds on television advertising.

My own fascination with political paper advertising surfaced during the 1960 presidential campaign between John Kennedy and Richard Nixon. For some reason, I felt compelled to save every sample ballot, booklet, bumper sticker, brochure, pamphlet, poster, and hand-out I could get my hands on. When the election was over, my scrapbook was filled and my dollar investment was zero.

Of course, no one really expected the paper material to be worth much in the years ahead. It was designed to be distributed during the heat of the presidential campaign and then discarded, which is exactly what most people who came in contact with it did. Win or lose, they trashed their campaign paper once the votes were in.

A great deal of political advertising paper was produced over the years in amazing quantities, but few people saved or preserved it. Much of what did survive is now collectible.

The other thing that happened to political advertising paper, especially the presidential election part of it, was television. Sure, some presidential candidates may pass out a few brochures here and there, but most of the millions and millions of dollars spent on elections is strictly for the electronic media. Since the 1970s, TV advertising has consumed about 95 cents of every presidential campaign dollar. It is no wonder that even once-common bumper stickers are scarce. (Have you noticed that some are now mounted inside, on the passenger side of the rear window, and not on the outside bumper?)

Republican Ticket.

For President, ... ULYSSES S. GRANT.
For Vice-President, . . SCHUYLER COLFAX.

OUR COUNTRY AND ITS DEFENDERS.

I propose to move immediately upon your works.—*Grant*

For Electors of President and Vice-President,

AMOS PAUL,   South-Newmarket
JOEL EASTMAN,   *144*   Conway
MASON W. TAPPAN,   Bradford
EDWARD L. GODDARD, Claremont
ALBERT M. SHAW,   Lebanon

Republican Ticket for Grant and Colfax; black on white paper. (Hake's Americana, York, PA)

Reagan-Bush campaign poster, 1984. (Hake's Americana, York, PA)

During the latter nineteenth century, supporters of leading presidential candidates really had two sources of paper materials. One was the campaign itself, and the other was the commercial marketplace, where it sometimes seemed like a good idea to link a product with the candidates.

Trade cards were a good example. (More on trade cards in general in chapter 13).

Some trade cards flatly favored one presidential candidate over another. In 1884, a trade card from Muzzy's Starch congratulated the ticket of James Blaine and John Logan, although the eventual winner was Grover Cleveland. Four years later, the Merrick Thread Company added a little romance to the campaign with a trade card depicting former bachelor and President Grover Cleveland and his lovely, young bride Frances Folsom Cleveland. They had been married in the White House, and the trade card added that Merrick Thread was "the thread that binds the Union." Despite the nice card, Cleveland lost that year to Benjamin Harrison.

Of course, many other trade cards attempted to play things right down the middle. In 1876, for example, Blackwell's Durham Tobacco issued cards for both Samuel Tilden and U.S. Grant. In 1888, the Catalin Tobacco Company issued a card with the 1884 electoral votes for James Blaine on one side, and the 1884 electoral votes for Cleveland on the other. Smokers were asked to check off the states they expected their candidate to carry in '88. Likewise, during the hotly contested election of 1900, a company selling Presidential Suspenders issued a colorful card with Miss Columbia holding out suspenders to presidential candidates William McKinley and William Jennings Bryan. On the back of each card, customers were urged to guess the popular vote of the election.

Another "commercial" source of political advertising paper during the nineteenth century was the legendary Currier and Ives. In 1844, Currier and Ives provided a hand-tinted poster for the Grant National Whig party featuring the images of Henry Clay and Theodore

Mondale campaign poster, 1984. (Hake's Americana, York, PA)

Frelinghuysen. Over the years, the company did at least 15 different lithographic portraits of Clay, who ran unsuccessfully for president three times. During the presidential campaign of 1860, the company provided prints for three major candidates—Republican Abe Lincoln, Democrat John Breckenridge, and Constitutional Union Party Choice John Bell.

Currier and Ives "did not take sides in such controversies," according to Ewell Newman in *A Guide to Collecting Currier & Ives*. "Portraits of the three presidential aspirants and banners promoting their candidacies rolled from the Currier and Ives presses in response to sectional enthusiasms." The print makers continued providing portraits and banners for presidential choices up to the first administration of Cleveland in the 1880s.

Beyond trade cards and Currier and Ives prints, newspapers and magazines are another source of political advertising paper that was around in the nineteenth century and expanded into the twentieth century. Serious collectors can select from an 1801 issue of the *Boston Gazette* which carried Thomas Jefferson's inaugural address, or an 1856 copy of *Frank Leslie's Illustrated* which bore John C. Fremont, the first presidential candidate of the Republican party, on the cover.

Possibly the most famous election-related newspaper of the twentieth century was the classic *Chicago Tribune* from the 1948 campaign erroneously proclaiming that Thomas Dewey had defeated Harry Truman. Adding to the story, and the collectibility of the newspaper, is a famous photograph of beaming presidential victor Harry Truman hold-ing up the very newspaper from his speaking podium. Though that particular newspaper can, and does, command prices up to several hundred dollars, most twentieth century newspapers related to the presidential campaigns can still be readily found at reasonable rates. Various news magazines also fit well into this category.

Much harder to find are the catalogs of the late nineteenth century and the early twentieth century which offered special selections of campaign goods. In 1880, Lippincott Company in Chicago advertised materials for both Chester Arthur and James Garfield. Their colorful ad listed bunting, streamers, badges, five-foot torches, and even suits for the marching campaign officer.

Silver print of Harry Truman holding "Dewey Defeats Truman" edition of the *Chicago Tribune*, in 1948. It was wrong. Frank Cancellare photo. (Swann Galleries collection)

Catalog page for presidential campaign uniforms and materials; Lippincott Company, 1880.

Sheet music "The Sidewalks of New York," official Al Smith campaign issue, 1928.

Lyndon Johnson presidential postcard in full color, 1960s.

Sheet music from the 1940 presidential election saluting Franklin Roosevelt.

1940 Campaign Handbook, published for the Pure Oil Co.

Kennedy campaign poster, 1960. (Hake's Americana, York, PA)

Democratic Ticket, Cleveland/Hendricks, ca. 1884. (Hake's Americana, York, PA)

Political poster from the 1884 presidential campaign featuring the Cleveland/Hendricks ticket.

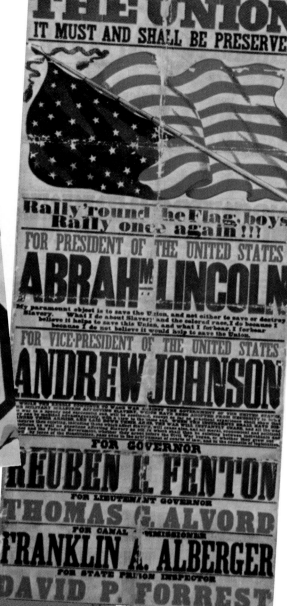

Poster featuring Abraham Lincoln in 1864 as National Unionist Presidential choice.

Political candidate card from 1882, for hand distribution to voters.

Campaign poster of 1900 makes extensive use of American flag motif.

William McKinley advertising card, presidential election, early twentieth century.

Taft postcard, 1907. (Hake's Americana, York, PA)

Vote for the Candidates of the Roosevelt Democracy in Pennsylvania

For United States Senator
JOSEPH F. GUFFEY ☒

For Governor
GEORGE H. EARLE ☒

For Lieutenant Governor
THOMAS KENNEDY ☒

For Secretary of Internal Affairs
THOMAS A. LOGUE ☒

For Superior Court Judge
CHESTER H. RHODES ☒

Primaries, Tuesday, May 15, 1934

FDR poll card for a 1934 primary election.
(Hake's Americana, York, PA)

Early twentieth-century sheet music for Teddy Roosevelt.

Harry Truman comic book from the 1948 presidential campaign.

Campaign poster from 1940, as FDR sought a third term.

Pathfinder magazine, Harry Truman cover, December 1950.

"I Like Ike" cigarettes, 1952. (Hake's Americana, York, PA)

A wide assortment of other presidential campaign paper also remains. It ranges from paper ballots, designed to expose voters to the full party ticket, to various brochures and booklets, and even to sheet music, postcards, posters and trading cards.

Sheet music has been an oddly important part of presidential campaigns for nearly two centuries. In 1828, the victors could shuffle to President Andrew Jackson's "Inauguration March For the Piano Forte." By 1888, they could step off to Benjamin Harrison's "Victory March" or warble "When Grover Goes Marching Home," an anti-Cleveland ditty. William Jennings Bryan supporters trotted out "The Farmer's Campaign Song" in 1908, while New York Governor Al Smith incorporated "The Sidewalks of New York" in his 1928 campaign. Both songs failed to elect their candidate, but both made interesting paper memorabilia as song sheets. In 1940, President Franklin Roosevelt's campaign joined the growing ranks with "We Can Win With Roosevelt." "We can win with Roosevelt, he's best of all," it proclaimed. "So let's string-a-long and vote for him this fall."

Postcards were an already established medium of communication and commercial messages early in the twentieth century, so they naturally were adopted by political organizations. Sometimes the postcards offered slogans like one used for William Jennings Bryan in 1908, which described him as the "Man Who Made Lincoln Famous." That same year, William Howard Taft appeared on a postcard with incumbent president Theodore Roosevelt, who had endorsed him. Four years later, Roosevelt ran

![Kennedy-Johnson bumper sticker](KENNEDY JOHNSON)

CITIZENS FOR KENNEDY AND JOHNSON. 265 CONSTITUTION AVENUE, N.W., WASHINGTON, D.C.

Kennedy-Johnson bumper sticker from the 1960 presidential campaign.

Official campaign photo of the Kennedy family, 1960.

John F. Kennedy presidential campaign brochure, 1960, red, white, and blue.

Kennedy

Robert F. Kennedy campaign poster, 1968. (Hake's Americana, York, PA)

He's making us proud again.

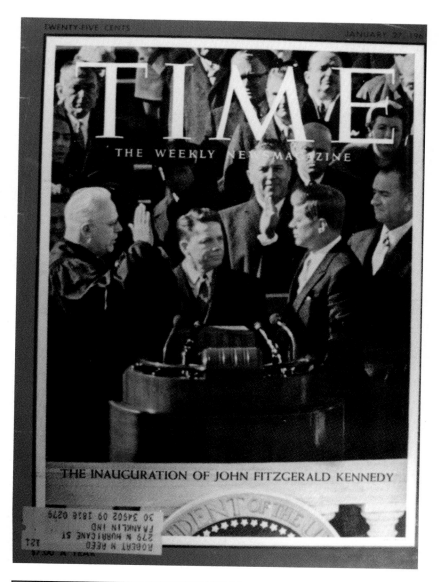

THE INAUGURATION OF JOHN FITZGERALD KENNEDY

Time magazine, coverage of the inauguration of JFK, 1961.

Left: Nixon campaign poster, 1972, Pennsylvania. (Hake's Americana, York, PA)

Far Left: Ford Campaign poster, 1976. (Hake's Americana, York, PA)

DIAL
NIXON 73
~ OR ~
# MI 9-6673
FOR VOTING INFORMATION
WEEKDAYS 10 A.M. to 4 P.M.
SATURDAYS 10 A.M. to 1 P.M.
~ COURTESY OF ~
REPUBLICAN COMMITTEE OF LOWER MERION AND NARBERTH

Brochures from presidential efforts of Ronald Reagan, Jimmy Carter, and Gerald Ford.

Ronald Reagan brochure for 1980 presidential campaign, in full color.

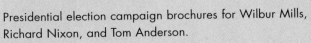

Presidential election campaign brochures for Wilbur Mills, Richard Nixon, and Tom Anderson.

Selection of political bumper stickers from Dukakis to Nixon Watergate reference to Reagan.

Presidential campaign bumper stickers for Buchanan, Reagan-Bush, and Brown.

against Taft on a third-party ticket. Campaign postcards continued to be popular into the 1960s, with the likes of John F. Kennedy, Lyndon B. Johnson, and Barry Goldwater sometimes promoting the candidates, and sometimes simply urging voters to the polls.

Booklets designed to inform uninformed voters were long a standard not only of campaigns but of merchants. In the 1880s, for example, it was not unusual for a "Political Information" booklet to be printed privately and filled with advertisements by local merchants, who offered everything from plumbing to undertaking. In 1940, the Pure Oil Company sponsored a campaign handbook as a premium for a nationally broadcast radio show. Even in the 1960s such booklets were frequently distributed under the sponsorship of regional or local merchants.

Generally, from the 1840s through the 1940s, various paper or cardboard ballots were distributed as campaign literature by various presidential supporters. Typically, these ballots included leading choices for the "party ticket" from presidential and vice presidential candidates on down. By their nature, they were usually state or regionally based, with relevant candidates or presidential electors listed. Today, they can still be found, and, compared to some other campaign memorabilia of the same period, are modestly priced.

Carter-Mondale, Dukakis-Bentsen, and Bush-Quayle presidential election bumper stickers.

Notes to Collectors:

Those with interest in political paper advertising can specialize in several areas:

• Collect items from a particular election—the presidential elections of 1972 or 1976 (the nation's bicentennial), for example.

• Collect from a specific century—the nineteenth or twentieth century—or a favored decade, such as the 1950s or 1960s.

• Collect presidential advertising paper from losing candidates or third party candidates such as George Wallace or Ross Perot.

• Seek items relating to a particular presidential winner, such as John F. Kennedy or Richard Nixon (these two are among the most popular with collectors who select a single candidate).

• Collect state or regional political advertising paper—from Texas, for example, or from the South.

Recommended for further reading:

Hake's Guide to Presidential Campaign Collectibles, by Ted Hake (Wallace-Homestead).

Official Price Guide to Political Memorabilia, by Richard Friz (House of Collectibles).

political advertising paper values:

BOOKLETS

Anti-FDR, Frankie in Wonderland, 1934, 24 pages, 5" x 8", character drawings . .$62

Pure Oil Company, Kaltenborn's 1940 Campaign Handbook $25

Kennedy: Leader of the 60's, 1960, presidential campaign issue, red,

white, and blue $35

BOOKMARK

Abraham Lincoln, July 1860, Lincoln-Hamlin ticket, 2 1/2" x 8 3/4", Journal &

Republican $385

BROCHURES

Time for Greatness, John F. Kennedy, 1960, red, white, and blue $11

Time is Now, Ronald Reagan, 1980, full color $4

Reasons for Reagan, 1980, full color $3

Jimmy Carter, 1976, green and white $3

Gerald Ford, 1976, blue and blue $3

Wilbur Mills, 1972, black and white $4

Re-elect the President, 1972, Richard Nixon $4

Tom Anderson, 1976, red, white, and blue $4

The Record, 1972, Richard Nixon, full color $5

Bill Clinton, 1992, red, white, and blue $2

Jimmy Carter and Walter Mondale jugate, 1976, green and white $4

BUMPER STICKERS

Kennedy-Johnson, 1960, red, white, and blue $34

Dukakis-Bentson, 1988, red and blue $2

Reagan, 1984, red, white, and blue $3

Nixon Bugs Me, 1974, Watergate related, black and orange $6

Buchanan for President, 1992, red, white, and blue $2

Reagan-Bush, 1984, red, white, and blue $3

Brown, 1992, blue and white $2

Dukakis-Bentsen, 1988, blue and white $3

Bush-Quale, 1988, red, white, and blue $3

Carter-Mondale, 1976, green and white $4

CARDS

Advertising card, William McKinley photo on pasteboard, early 1900s $8

Advertising card, Theodore Roosevelt, Rough Riders and Fairbank's Fairy Soap, 4" x 6" stiff cardboard, ca. 1898 . . . .$65

Advertising card, Rutherford Hayes, ca. 1878, paper card 3" x 4", Visit to Philadelphia, Potts Cold Handle Sad Irons $75

Advertising card, Alf Landon, 1936, Landon-Knox Out Roosevelt And the New Deal, 3 1/4" x 5 1/2" tan card, browned $30

Candidate business card, 1882, McGill for County Clerk, green with black type . . .$5

Poll card, 1934 primary election, photo of Franklin Roosevelt $20

CATALOG PAGE

Lippincott's Compliments to Garfield & Arthur Clubs, 1880, color ad for campaign uniforms and materials $18

CIGARETTES

"I Like Ike," cigarette package, 1952, red, white, and blue $75

COMIC BOOKS

John Kennedy, PT 109, 1964, glossy cover, 32 pages, some creasing and browning $27

The Story of Harry Truman, 1948, full color $35

FANS

Who Will Be Next? 1928, inset of presidents, reverse hardware store advertisement $55

Robert Taft, Win With Taft, 1952, red, green, and white cardboard $23

HANDBILL

Richard Nixon, 1972 inaugural parade, photos, route, and dates, red, white, and blue $16

NEEDLE BOOK

Herbert Hoover, 1928, Stick to the Republican Party, photos of Hoover and Curtis .$22

MAGAZINES

Time magazine, John Kennedy 1961 inauguration $15

Pathfinder, Harry Truman 1950 cover $8

PHOTOGRAPHS

Kennedy family, 1960, official campaign photo, black and white glossy $30

Truman holding mistaken *Chicago Tribune*, 1948, original silver print by

Frank Cancellare $1,540

POSTCARDS

Thomas Dewey, Do We Want Dewey, 1940, two elephants at Philadelphia Zoo . . .$65

Wm. Howard Taft, New England States for Taft, 1907, *Chicago Tribune* poll . . . $40

Warren Harding, 1915, photo with campaign in Ohio, browntone, unused

but creasing $48

Lyndon Johnson, 1964, full color photograph $5

Taft & Sherman, a winning pair, 1908, photos and flags $28

Richard Nixon, Checkers speech, 1952, Dear Friend thank you message,

black and white glossy $34

POSTERS

Anti-Stevenson, 1952, Don't Let This Happen to You, Vote for Ike, 6" x 14",

stiff orange paper $55

Shirley Chisholm, 1972, Bring Us Together, 11 1/2" x 14 1/2", cardboard, red,

white, and blue $45

National Unionist campaign, 1864, Abraham Lincoln and Andrew Johnson,

full color $9,780

Cleveland-Hendricks ticket, 1884, Democratic nominees, full color $385

W. J. Bryan, 1900, full color with American flag $307

Kennedy campaign poster, 1960, red, white, and blue, 13" x 20" $60

Ford campaign poster, 1976, full-color photo, 15" x 25" $20

Goldwater Victory Rally, 1964, Madison Square Garden, 13" x 22", red, white,

and blue, creases and soiling $30

Mondale campaign poster, 1984, National Education Association, 14" x 20" $16

Roosevelt campaign poster, 1940, A gallant leader, red, white, and blue $204

Reagan-Bush campaign poster, 1980, jugate $30

Nixon campaign, 1972, in Pennsylvania, 14" x 22" $30

Bobby Kennedy campaign, 1968, red and blue, 24" x 36" $70

SHEET MUSIC

"Teddy-Te-Tum-Tum-Tay," early twentieth century, for Teddy Roosevelt $85

"Sidewalks of New York," 1928, Al Smith cover $35

"We Can Win With Roosevelt," 1940, Roosevelt-Wallace jugate cover $23

SHOPPING BAG

Alf Landon, 1936, heavy brown paper, 17" x 17", campaign slogans, Vote
   for Landon $32

TICKETS

Democratic Ticket, 1884, Cleveland-Hendricks and state electors, 3" x 5" $44
Republican Ticket, 1868, Grant illustrated, with electors listed $75

chapter ten
advertising postcards

*"You can tell the ideas of a nation
by its advertisements."*
Norman Douglas, 1917

The story of advertising postcards is still ongoing. Unlike so many other areas of paper advertising collectibles, such postcards are still very much in use more than a century after they first appeared. At our house, they turn up all the time from auction houses, the dentist, antique shows, the telephone company, and the veterinarian.

To a large extent, advertising has been the single driving force in the long life of the American postcard itself. Far beyond mere pleasant greetings or pleasing views, these particular commercial postcards have been used to directly sell products and services for more than 100 years now, and are still going strong. That puts them in a fairly elite group.

Moreover, their century-plus of service has given the collector some of the most treasured examples of print advertising ever seen. In fact, such gems as Coca-Cola and Campbell's Soup advertising postcards have been admired and sought since they were first introduced.

Part of the reason that advertising postcards were so immediately successful was because, in the public's mind, they were so similar to trade cards which were the rage of the late nineteenth century.

Postcards also had an added advantage—not only did they have much of the dazzle and directness of trade cards, but they could be mailed, as well as simply passed out to customers. For a relatively low cost, the merchant or manufacturer could send cards *enmasse* to specific audiences, such as regular customers living in a particular area. Thus, the postcards became a tool of targeted advertising before the term itself was ever known.

Early 1900s advertising postcard for Milton Ochs Clothes, in color.

Coca-Cola ad postcard for bottled drink, 1910.

Campbell's Soup trade card, early twentieth century.

This is not to say they became more popular than trade cards. They did not. This is not to say they were issued in greater numbers than trade cards. They were not. But they did immediately appeal to the public, and were just as quickly collected.

By the dawn of the twentieth century, however, things had changed in the advertising world. Trade cards had all but disappeared, yet advertising postcards had come into their own as a strong positive force in American enterprise. Some would contend they have never really lost that role.

Coca-Cola was one of the first national manufacturers to see the tremendous potential in postcard advertising. As early as 1905, they not only had put their regional bottling plants on postcards for distribution, they also offered cards showing attractive people with their product as well. The Duster girl, a woman in a striking hat driving an automobile, appeared on behalf of Coca-Cola as early as 1906. Later, there were more plants, delivery vehicles, women wearing fashionable hats, and even school teachers.

Around 1913, Coke issued a nifty advertising postcard with the planet earth on it. Their "All Over The World" message read as follows:

"You will find Coca-Cola signs that create a demand you must supply.

Don't miss the chance.

It's the sign of prosperity."

Not exactly Emily Dickinson, but these powerful little postcards were clearly getting the message across. During the 1940s, Coke issued a set of four postcards which incorporated the image of comic-hero crime fighter Dick Tracy. At the time, the postcards were issued as a sales promotion for those serving the U.S. in military forces. They are, of course, considered quite collectible by an assortment of groups, including those who fancy Dick Tracy memorabilia, Coke item collectors, and those who are generally attracted to advertising postcards of all types.

The Campbell Soup Company and their chubby-faced Campbell Soup kids also made an early-on national impact via advertising postcards. During the early twentieth century the Kids first appeared as trolley cards in more than 300 of the nation's cities. Drawn by Grace Gebbie Wiederseim, the Kids were immediately popular, and they eventually appeared on postcards. Typically, the cards boasted the soup price of only ten cents a can, various slogans, and—best of all—the Kids were illustrated in full color. It is estimated that nearly a million of the cards were produced between 1912 and 1913.

Banner Buggy Co. postcard by R.F. Outcault, 1903, signed.

Early ad postcard for grocery store, January 1893.

Indois Hotel in downtown Terre Haute, IN, ca. 1918. Advertises "Welcome Stranger."

Postcard issued in both Titanic and Olympic names, before and after the sinking.

Postcard promotes historic play in Deadwood, South Dakota. Undated.

Green Valley Camp: Running water in every cabin. Canada, 1949.

Bicos' Lo-Bo Cafe. Wausau, Wisconsin, ca. 1930s.

Texaco service station advertising postcard, 1940. Lawson Wood, artist.

Speaking of the famous Kids, the artist herself once commented, "My children possess all the wisdom adults lose. With children acting as my medium I can be as sardonic or as ironic about things as I please and no one minds. Children get away with murder and so do I, the artist, get the message across with them." (A note about that famed artist's signature: Due to her multiple marriages, her signed works can also be found with the last names of Gebbie and Drayton.)

As early as 1887, Roberts, Parry, and Company were using advertising postcards to help promote and sell their stoves. Similar formats were later followed by Murray Buggy Manufacturing Company, and the Seamless Steel Tubing Company of Boston, Massachusetts. By the 1890s, even small grocery stores were making use of cards to make customers aware of their "best buys."

In the early 1900s, advertising postcards included an appealing one depicting a little girl and a tray from Schlitz Beer saying, "Mamma Says It Keeps Us All Well," and a factory scene from J. Krauss and Company Machines. Other nifty examples included a picture of the Panama Canal from Hostetter's Stomach Bitters, and a mother and daughter together on behalf of McKee High Grade Refrigerators. Meanwhile, legendary comic strip artist Richard F. Outcault contributed to advertisements and, in turn, to ad postcards early in the twentieth century with such creations as the Yellow Kid and Buster Brown. Outcault's work promoted numerous companies around the country, including the Banner Buggy Company in St. Louis, Missouri.

H.J. Heinz used full-color postcards to tout food produce in the early 1900s, including baked beans, tomato soup, mincemeat, and dill pickles. N.K. Fairbanks used the Gold Dust Twins on postcards (as well as on other items) for soap products as early as 1910. Just a year later, the Ford Motor Company captured America's attention with a form-changing advertising postcard folder featuring their newest automobile. Steward Iron Fence offered a mechanical advertising postcard soon afterward—in which a flap folded down to replace an illustrated wooden fence with an illustrated iron one.

A little romance came into play when Hires used advertising postcards in 1912. The soft

Postcard from 1940s depicting Uncle Sam's image.

Patriotic postcard issued by the U.S. Treasury Dept., ca. 1943.

Tom Breneman's Breakfast in Hollywood radio show postcard, Kellogg Co., 1945.

Brink Bingo Supplies, red lettering on white card, 1949.

drink company tried a personal message from an imaginary character to boost the sale of root beer. "Dear Jack," read the scripted message on the back of each postcard, "Be sure and come early this evening. I made root beer from Hires household extract, the kind you like so well and it is delicious. You must drink a lot of it to get as rosy cheeks as, Yours affectionately Alice." Those root beer cards signed so affectionately by Alice, with her lively image on the front, proved to be a hit with the public and are well-known to collectors today.

Kellogg's provided mechanical advertising postcards during the late 1930s and early 1940s which had swing-out panels that depicted Snap, Crackle, and Pop of Rice Krispies fame. Harley-Davidson, meanwhile, issued a number of dealer-based postcards at around the same time, inviting the public to view the new models. For the more exotic-minded, there were advertising postcards calling customers to gambling ships off the coast of California also during the 1930s and 1940s. Among them were Johanna Smith's World Famous Gambling Ship, featuring roulette and slot machines.

The 1939 World's Fair in New York City saw a record number of promotional and advertising postcards from exhibitors at that event. Among the most prominent were DuPont, Ford Motor Company, and the Borden Company, which

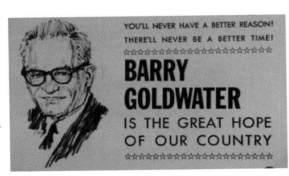

Political advertising postcard for Goldwater presidential campaign, 1964.

B R I D G E
ILLUSION IN CLAY

Ad postcard for Smithsonian Institution, Sackler Gallery, 5 1/2" x 8 1/2".

issued packs of postcards starring Elsie the Cow. Just months before the outbreak of World War II, General Motors issued a full-color advertising postcard featuring the 1941 Buick. The postcard asked prospective customers, "Know How Little This One Costs?"

During the 1950s, automobiles continued to be a favored topic of ad postcards, including the Nash Airflyte, the Plymouth Belvedere Sport Coup, the two-door Edsel sedan, and the Rambler Super Cross Country station wagon. In the decades that followed, market-wise advertisers like McDonald's, Sears, and JC Penney—among others—have added to the color and diversity of advertising postcard collectibles.

Advertising postcards were very much a twentieth century thing—and to a large extent, the twentieth century was very much an advertising postcard thing.

Notes to Collectors:

There are three possible ways to determine the date of advertising postcards:
• In some cases, the date or copyright date is part of the printed image.
• Postmarks can show when a postcard was mailed, and generally indicate pretty much when it was issued.
• Postage applied to the back of the postcard can be helpful. From the 1870s until 1917 the cost of sending a card was one cent. The price was raised to two cents for a brief time and returned to one cent from 1919 until 1925. The price of the penny postcard did not go to two cents until 1953, and was three cents from 1959 until 1963.

CR-V Honda automobile advertising postcard, 1997. Sepia browntone.

advertising postcard values:

Barber-Coleman Company, model E tying machine, real photo $30

Banner Buggy Company, 1905, R.F. Outcaut artist $12

Bicos' Lo-Bo Cafe, ca. 1930s, restaurant interior, color photo, Wausau, Wisconsin . $3

Buick dealer, ca. 1938, "great 5-passenger special sedan model 41" pictured,
   sepia card $20

Tom Breneman's "Breakfast in Hollywood" radio show, 1945, from Kellogg Co. . .$8

Brink Bingo Supplies, 1949, red lettering $5

Campbell Soups, unsigned artist Grace Wiederseim, numbered $33

Cowboy Antiques, 1991, show and auction, Cody, Wyoming, color photo
   of memorabilia $1

Cunard Line Ocean Steamer, sepia R.M.S. Aquitania, ca. 1920s, unused $20

Dupont's Powder, full-color image of people and wagon, artist Howard Pyle $15

Elgin Watch Co., 1914, costumed youngster $40

Milton Ochs Clothes, ca. 1906, depicts Alaskan miner, full color $12

Cabin Creek Coal Sales, depicts Uncle Sam saying "Buy coal now," ca. 1940s $4

Economy King Cream Separators, 1916, Sears, Roebuck and Company $65

Garner For President Committee, business reply card, black and white,
   Dallas, Texas $6

Gold Dust Twins, 1910, cartoon image for soap products, N.K. Fairbanks
   and Company $22

Barry Goldwater, 1964, Republican presidential candidate depicted, black and
   white sketch $8

Green Valley Camp, 1939, running water in every cabin, black and white photo,
   Ottawa, Canada $4

Heinz Company ocean pier, ca. 1910, Atlantic City attraction $8

Honda automobile, CR-V model, sepia browntone card $1

Howard Johnson restaurant, ca. 1950s, aerial photo, black and white,
   Pennsylvania Turnpike $4

Lemaux Brothers Groceries, 1893, with dry good prices $12

Hires Root Beer, 1912, message from Alice, black script $18

Harley-Davidson motorcycles, 1935, message to customers from dealer $24

Indois Hotel, ca. 1918, "Welcome Stranger," color photo of hotel and street scene . . $6

Nabisco, ca. 1900, full color, Home of Shredded Wheat, unused $12

U.S. Bank Safe Company, ca. 1930s, illustrated $7

U.S. Treasury Department, ca. 1943, Buy More War Bonds, waving soldier, full color $2

Sakewitz, McMillan & Bowman cheese and creamery butter, ca. 1920, warehouse order card $4

Spiegel mail order catalog, 1928, mail reply for "bargain book" $3

Silvertone Phonographs, ca. 1920, from Sears, Roebuck and Company $65

Skinner, Inc. 1995, auction gallery, color photo of eighteenth century Kiddush cups .$1

Smithsonian Institution, Sackler Gallery, 1997, Bridge Illusion In Clay exhibition .$1

Texaco Service Station, 1940, chimp cartoon by artist Lawson Wood, includes monthly calendar $6

Tony The Tiger, 1966, cartoon image, Kellogg's Cereals $6

Trial of Jack McCall for Killing Wild Bill Hickok, ca. 1940s, nightly stage play in Deadwood, South Dakota, red card depicts Wild Bill $5

Swann Galleries poster auction, 1993, depicts example from New York World's Fair, all color $2

White Star Line, ca. 1912, T.S.S. Titanic depicted, full color $145

chapter eleven
advertising posters

*"Few people can make money while they sleep,
but put old paper away to sleep and it increases
in value with the passing of each day and year."*
Morgan Towne,
author of *Treasures in Truck and Trash*

When author Morgan Towne was writing such optimistic things about paper collectibles, he was actually making specific references at the time to advertising posters. The book was a small volume entitled, *Treasures in Truck and Trash.* The year was 1947.

Understand that Towne was publishing his views at a time when the post-war United States had just cleaned the shelves and closets of most paper from the past for scrap drives. Not only had Americans been happy to assist the war effort, they were also happy to rid themselves of worthless old newspapers, almanacs, calendars, catalogs, magazines, and, of course, any dusty old advertising posters.

Decades before the experts of the 1980s and 1990s came along to make saving stuff fashionable, here was Towne with an apparent straight face telling people that posters may honestly have some value. If not on that date, then certainly in the years to come. At one point, he noted that posters dealing with anything scientific, even household tools, were worth saving and preserving. Moreover, he flatly stated that

World War I poster, by James Montgomery Flagg.

posters advertising songsters, tumblers, minstrels, or nearly anything theatrical was like "finding money in the bank." Towne went on to say that movie posters featuring Mary Pickford, Charlie Chaplin, and Harold Lloyd were already valued, and most any movie, museum, or circus poster from the 1920s and 1930s would take on considerable value "in another 20 or 30 years."

It turns out, of course, that Towne was very prophetic, at least when the subject concerned advertising on paper. Bear in mind, he was writing at a time when a poster advertising the 1859 execution of John Brown was going for around $100 in very good condition. A broadside poster advertising the stage play presentation of Shakespeare's *Richard III*, in 1818 in Baltimore, Maryland, was available for a mere $18.

The wonderful world of advertising posters has been contributing to the commercial scene for well over a century. Today, posters of all ages are collectible.

Rising from the plainly lettered broadsides of the middle-nineteenth century, posters went on to become what many experts consider the most refined advertising art available. As author John Mebane explains in *New Horizons in Collecting*, "American poster advertising during the last quarter of the nineteenth century was largely devoted to the circus and theatrical events; however, since the first quarter of the twentieth century, posters have been used to advertise thousands of articles or merchandise, and scores of services."

Certainly a favored few colorful posters have managed to outlive all the products, productions, and special events they sought to proclaim and advertise.

Possibly the ultimate in collectible posters are the original works of French artists of the 1890s such as Alphonse Mucha, Henri Toulouse-Lautrec, and Jules Cheret. Their characters and colors remain the ultimate in Art Nouveau poster design.

Colorful poster by French artist Jules Cheret, 1893, La Loie Fuller. (Swann Galleries Photo)

In the Indianapolis area they tell the story of a young man who was visiting Paris one evening in 1899. After a series of performances, George Alexander Clowes walked into one leading theater and helped himself to a larger-than-life poster of the then-beloved actress Sarah Bernhardt. He was attracted to the swirling bands of color which had been the work of Alphonse Mucha, but in reality he saved the distinguished poster from removal and destruction by the building's work crew. During his lifetime, Clowes went on to become one of the leading citizens of Indianapolis. The fantastic Art Nouveau poster is now part of the permanent collection of the Indianapolis Museum of Art.

Most of us will not be fortunate enough to spot one of the great French artists on the playhouse wall (if you do, tip the work crew a couple of hundred for letting you "clean-up" and vanish. A nice lithograph poster of Sarah Bernhardt, done by Mucha, would bring $3,500 or more in today's market.) but there certainly are other posters, other times, and other walls to consider. The full range of collectible advertising posters extends vastly to a host of artists, topics, and artistic periods of history.

Because posters were such a mammoth advertising medium, the extent of subjects depicted since the late nineteenth century is vast. Collectors can focus on everything from airplanes and automobiles to tobacco and world's fairs and expositions.

In the early days, broadside posters were simply printed words, oftentimes using different sizes and styles of type. It was not until after the Civil War that advertisers began to see any real advantage in using images and graphics with their posted advertising messages.

The development of the trade card and the breathless full-blown color chromolithography that came with them was also highly instrumental in influencing manufacturers and merchants to go further. By the 1870s, the marketplace was awash in stunning and ever-developing printing processes. It just made sense to use the startling images on full-blown advertising posters.

Actually, many historians feel that some of the emerging posters of the latter nineteenth century were simply over-sized trade cards. Most trade cards of the time were printed on light-weight card stock; however, some were printed on what was relatively thin paper. Advertisers and printers then proceeded to use the thinner paper for larger but still colorful images. They moved from cards to flyers, handbills, broadsides, and posters.

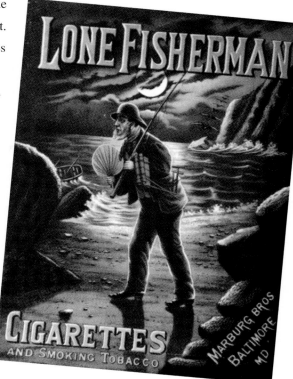

Advertising poster for Lone Fisherman Cigarettes, ca. 1880s, lithographed.

Back in 1969, author Louis Hertz thought the connection was so obvious that "the collecting of all these is at once a separate hobby in itself, or at least a distinct category of advertising antiques." Hertz added in *Antique Collecting for Men* that some items were "also an essential segment of catalog collecting, many early manufacturers issued only a single sheet describing and promoting their lines."

As lithography advanced into the 1880s and beyond, so did the ability of the printers to produce varied posters. Moreover, leading companies such as Currier and Ives, Louis Prang, and Julius Bein were able to offer customized ad posters using stock artwork—much as had been done with some greeting cards and lots of trade cards.

While some posters were certainly specially prepared and printed, a great many (like their sister trade cards) simply had final details added to stock designs. Good examples of these in late nineteenth-

Lithograph Fair poster, 1892, Carson, Nevada.

Political poster, "Our Friend," by Ben Shahn, 1944. For the Franklin Roosevelt presidential campaign.

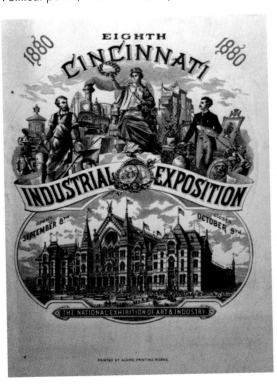

Nineteenth-century poster for Industrial Exposition in Cincinnati, Ohio, 1880.

Poster for seed catalog of B.K. Bliss & Sons Company, intended to be placed in stores, 1880, color.

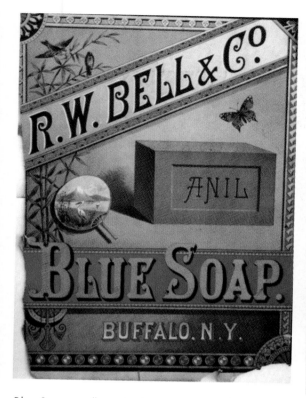

Blue Soap cardboard advertising poster from R.W. Bell & Co., 1880s, lithographed.

Poster for the Great Holman, 1909, published by the Courier Co. of Buffalo, New York. (Skinner Inc. auction photo)

Poster of World War I era by Harrison Fisher, championing the Red Cross.

Colorful, striking World War I poster for Liberty Bonds, F. Strothmann artist.

Lithographed poster promoting Kar-Mi magic show, from 1914.

century posters were country fair and race-meet type posters. Frequently, in cases like this, very attractive and multicolored posters were simply imprinted with the name and date of the local event to be featured. This is a practice that apparently confused some early collectors, according to Hertz, "who were often puzzled to find identical posters advertising events many miles and months apart." Thus, the dashing harness race horses at the 1892 Ormsby County Fair in Nevada can also be the very same handsome trotters advertising the harness races at the Ohio State Fair that same year. Both were provided by the Calvert Lithographic Company of Detriot, Michigan.

Still another good example were posters for traveling theater shows during the last two decades of the nineteenth century. "The advertising (poster sheets) announced the name of the company, the date of engagement, and the title of the first play," notes Harlow Hoyt in the comprehensive volume, *Town Hall Tonight*. "It was illustrated with a prison escape, a buzzsaw rescue, a duel with knives, or some other situation adapted to lithographic reproduction. Further than that it did not go."

Other posters, however, did go further, including those of the traveling circus. Like acting troupes, the traveling circuses went from town to town and generally slapped up their richly colored promotion posters wherever they could. Among the most aggressive circus bands of the late nineteenth century was that of W.C. Coup, one of the pioneers in developing the use of flatcars to rapidly move circus operations by rail.

According to legend, Coup and his crew were visiting various towns and pasting up W.C. Coup Circus posters one summer when they came upon a new theater which had just completed a run of William Shakespeare's works. An image of the great playwright and his accomplishments was located in a prominent place. Upon being informed that the spot was sort of a tribute, Coup quipped:

"Shakespeare? Never heard of him. Paint him out and paste up a picture poster of the W.C. Coup Circus."

Barnum and Bailey's Greatest Show on Earth was among those most profoundly promoted around the country in posters of lavish and enduring color. Stunningly illustrated circus posters created by Strobridge Lithography in Cincinnati, Ohio, during the 1890s remain vivid and treasured today.

There were, of course, many other circus operations and resulting posters from Clyde Beatty and Cole Brothers to Sells and Wallace Brothers. Typically, circus posters were printed in a standard 28" x 42" size. A half sheet could be 14" x 42" or 28" x 21". Usually the sizes could then be combined for giant banner scenes for large walls or even barns. There were, however, exceptions to the standard sizes, even with Barnum and Bailey.

Still another highly impressive area of late nineteenth century and early twentieth century posters were those that proclaimed and promoted professional displays of magic. Some of the finest magic posters were, not surprisingly, produced by Strobridge Litho, which also had championed circus posters. Other "magic makers" included Othis Lithography Company, National Printing and Engraving Company, Donaldson Lithography, Great Western, Friedlander, and Russell-Morgan. All of the great magicians of that time used their great skills to advertise in clear, bright, and enduring detail—Houdini, Carter the Great, Chung Ling Soo, Howard Thurston, Kar-Mi, Harry Kellar, Servais Le Roy, and Grover George.

Early twentieth-century lithographed posters dealing with World War I are also moving and unforgettable. Some were patriotically penned by leading artists of the day, while others were contributed by relatively unknown talents. Howard Chandler Christy provided a number of highly popular and widely used recruiting posters using alluring women and gender bending themes, including "I Wish I Were A Man—I'd Join the Navy."

James Montgomery Flagg's poster work was equally prolific during WWI, with such efforts as "Together We Win" featuring both military and civilian workers. His famous offering of Uncle Sam pointing a finger and saying, "I Want You," is considered by many to be the most famous poster in America. (It was so popular, in fact, that revisions of it were used generations later during World War II.)

World War I poster by Howard Chandler Christy.

During World War II, in the 1940s, the American sweep of conflict-related posters was even greater than it had been in the previous war. Observed author John Mebane some years later in the book, *Collecting Nostalgia*:

Parkside's Chocolate Covered Honeycomb, ca. 1920, 20" x 14". (Swann Galleries photo)

Above Right: Light Consumes Coal, Save Light, Save Coal. Poster ca. 1915, by Coles Phillips, for the U.S. Fuel Administration.

Lithographed poster featuring Thurston's vanishing automobile, 1928. (Swann Galleries photo)

Colorful Macy's back-to-school poster, 1929, New York City.

Combined circus shows, Ringling Bros and Barnum & Bailey, ca. 1930s, full color.

Movie poster, *Son of Frankenstein*, ca. 1930s. (Swann Galleries photo)

1932 movie poster for Disney's *Whoopee Party*. © Walt Disney Company.

Coca-Cola poster from 1949. © Coca-Cola Company.

Cowboy and Coke, 1941 poster.
© Coca-Cola Company.

Book Week poster by artist Maurice Sendak, 1960, full color.

Right: Wallace Brothers Circus poster, 28" x 41", ca. 1950s, full color.

Drive-In movie poster, ca. 1964, multiple colors.

Bowery Boys stock stage show poster, 1964,
6" x 9", red, yellow, and black.

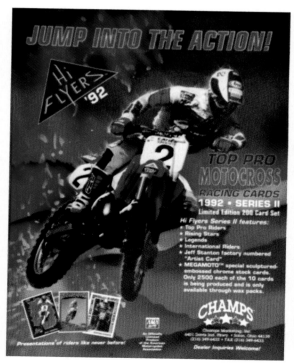

Professional motocross racing poster for trading
cards, issued by Champs Publishing.

Poster salutes collector cards based on the works of
artist Maxfield Parrish.

Kellogg's Krumbles poster, ca. 1915, printed on linen, 28" x 18". (Swann Galleries photo)

Right: World War I bond drive poster featuring the Boy Scouts of America, by J.C. Leyendecker.

"Thousands of posters, on the bulletin boards or walls of factories engaged in defense production, warned workers of the dangers of careless talk. Blood, of course, was urgently needed in treating the wounded, and a diversity of posters solicited blood donors—and, of course, there were recruiting posters galore. There were illustrations of soldiers under fire, soldiers praying, aviators, generals, and admirals. Many posters were issued under the auspices of the War Production Board, Office of War Information, and Office of Civilian Defense."

During both world wars of the twentieth century a great many posters were created for "official" use such as recruiting and information. Many others were made available directly to the public. Some posters of this nature were sold at patriotic rallies and parades, while others were retailed at novelty and gift shops. Hundreds of different kinds of war effort posters were produced for both historic periods, and, as a result, collectors were gathering them even before hostilities had ended in either war. Beyond military causes, collecting categories regularly featured at leading shows, galleries, and auction houses include animals, Art Nouveau, Art Deco, bicycles, cinema, fashion, magic, opera, Olympics, products, ships, skiing, sports, travel, and a growing number of specialties.

Products and services can be just about anything offered during the twentieth century in which the advertising medium was a striking and well-preserved poster. Gems range from Butter-Nut Bread and Kellogg's Krumbles, to Railway Express, the French-made Lucifer Bicycles, and Winchester Athletic Equipment.

Favored artists are also still a major source of poster collecting—not only in the United States, but in other countries as well. A number of nations, including Australia, France, Great Britain, Spain, and Switzerland, have contributed notable, and now highly collectible, poster artists.

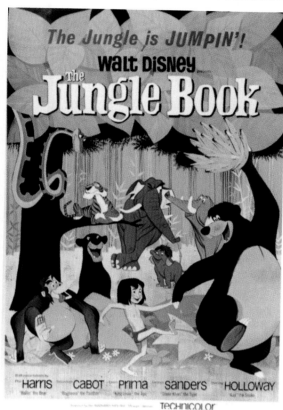

The Jungle is JUMPIN'!
WALT DISNEY The Jungle Book

Harris CABOT Prima SANDERS HOLLOWAY

TECHNICOLOR

One sheet movie poster, "The Jungle Book," 1967. © Walt Disney Company.

Among American artists whose posters are prized are John Atherton, R.F. Babcock, Jose Binder, Will Bradley, Charles Livingston Bull, Austin Cooper, J.C. Leyendecker, Winsor McCay, Blanche McManus, Edward Penfield, Coles Philips, Louis Rhead, Ben Shahn, Wilbur Macy Stone, and N.C. Wyeth.

In addition to the traditional artists and topics of the past, many posters of relatively recent issue have been appearing in the marketplace. The growing number of "new" subjects include Disney, cartoon videos, fast-food restaurants, holiday events, public health and social causes, *Star Wars*, trading cards, brand name clothing, women's sports, contemporary movies and re-releases of classic movies.

Even bread can have appeal as a poster topic, if properly done. In past years, one of a series of advertising posters promoting Levy Bread was included in the auction listings of the distinguished Swann Galleries in New York City. The poster, "You Don't Have to Be Jewish To Love Levy's Real Jewish Rye," featuring a Native American, proved, according to Swann, "that not only could an inspired poster bring a customer closer to a product, it could also bring Americans closer to each other." The poster sold for more than $600.

One leading U.S. collector and dealer of posters suggests you simply find posters you are going to enjoy living with. (Good advice, I might add, for any advertising paper.) People who buy up posters quickly without thinking about living with their purchase as it is displayed upon the nearby walls, might soon have these posters back in the marketplace.

On the other hand, confides this same poster expert, "I have things I've had for 20 years that I wouldn't sell for anything. When it comes to posters, if you enjoy something, then you know ultimately it's a good investment."

JOIN THE ARMY AIR SERVICE BE AN AMERICAN EAGLE!
CONSULT YOUR LOCAL DRAFT BOARD, READ THE ILLUSTRATED BOOKLET AT ANY RECRUITING OFFICE, OR WRITE TO THE CHIEF SIGNAL OFFICER OF THE ARMY, WASHINGTON, D.C.

Poster for Army Air Service, ca. 1917, by Alpha Litho Co. artist Charles Livingston Bull.

advertising poster values:

Anti Cruelty Week (early animal rights), ca. 1930s, 28" x 21", Illinois Litho Co.,
Chicago $632

Associated News Service coverage of Wills-Firpo boxing match, 1924, 13" x 17",
matted $115

Barnum and Bailey Greatest Show on Earth, 1894, 27 1/2" x 27 1/2" Strobridge Lith.
Co., Cincinnati $1,500

B.K. Bliss & Sons Company poster for seed catalog, 1880, full color $28

Blot it Out with Liberty Bonds, 1918, handprint, 41" x 27" $155

Blue Soap, R.W. Bell Company, 1880s, full color, lithographed $42

Book Week poster, 1960, artist Maurice Sendak, full color $40

Bowery Boys On Stage, 1964, stock issue, red, yellow, and black, 6" x 9" $18

Coca-Cola cowboy and Coke, 1941, full color, some fading $385

Coca-Cola, woman aboard sailboat, 1949, full color $465

Daily Worker, ca. 1930s, promoting newspaper, red, white, and blue, thin cardboard,
11" x 13 1/4" $125

Dental Care Keeps Him on the Job, 1942, U.S. Government Printing Office,
12 1/2" x 9 1/2" $72

Devon Drive-In, ca. 1964, multiple colors $12

Mike Dukakis presidential campaign rally poster, 1988, bluetone photo, Pittsburgh,
Pennsylvania, rally, 11" x 16" $25

Elmore: Magician and Illusionist, 1922, stock poster, 29" x 22" $350

Exhibition of Science, Festival of Britain, 1951, Robin Day, 29" x 19 1/2" $450

Folies-Bergere, La Loie Fuller, 1893, artist Jules Cheret $2,195

Gee, I Wish I Were A Man, WW I poster by Howard Chandler Christy $2,750

Great Holman, 1909, Courier Co. of Buffalo, New York $325

Hi Flyers, Motocross Racing Cards, 1992, Champs Publishing $6

Industrial Exposition, 1880, Cincinnati, Ohio, black and white $120

I Summon You, 1917, Red Cross, artist Harrison Fisher, 39" x 29" $225

I Want You, 1917, James Montgomery Flagg, some taping, 40" x 30" $1,095

Jenny On The Job, 1943, Government Printing Office, 14" x 10" $65

Join The Army Air Service, Be An American Eagle, ca. 1917, Charles Livingston Bull,
27" x 20", Alpha Litho Co. $1,265

Join The Navy, the Service for Fighting Men, ca. 1917, R.F. Babcock, 39" x 28" $875

Jo-Jo, The Russian Dog-Faced Boy, 1886, Barnum Circus poster, matted,
7" x 4 3/4" $100

"The Jungle Book," 1967, Walt Disney movie poster, one sheet $850

Kar-Mi: Performing the most startling mystery of India, 1914, color lithographed,
27" x 40" $290

Kellogg's Krumbles, child with cereal, ca. 1915, 28" x 18", printed on linen $74

The True Mother Goose book, 1895, 20" x 14 1/2", Heliotype Ptg. Co. $1,035

Liberty Bonds, Beat back the Hun, WW I poster, artist F. Strothmann, full color   . $145

Light Consumes Coal, Save Light—Save Coal, 1915, artist Coles Phillips, U.S.

    Fuel Administration $175

The London Handbook magazine, 1897, 29 1/2" x 19 1/2" Iliffe & Son,

    London $258

Lone Fisherman Cigarettes, ca. 1880s, lithographed $125

Macy's back-to-school poster, 1929, full color, New York City $132

Maxfield Parrish Collector Cards, Comic Images, full color $10

National Agricultural Exposition at Kansas City, Missouri, 1887, 30" x 40", Krebs   . . .

    Lithographing, (restoration) $920

New York World's Fair, 1939, John Atherton, 30" x 19" $1,750

Ormsby County Agricultural Fair, 1892, harness race, full color lithographed   . . . $85

Our Friend, Franklin Roosevelt campaign poster, 1944, artist Ben Shahn $1,940

Parkside's Chocolate Covered Honeycomb, ca, 1920s, 20" x 14" $85

Red Man Tobacco, ca. 1940s, railroad conductor, minor creasing, 11" x 15 2/5"   . $110

Ringling Bros. and Barnum & Bailey Combined Shows, ca. 1930s,

    27 1/2" x 41 1/2" lithograph $990

RKO Pictures promotion of Joe Louis and Jersey Joe Walcott fight, 1946,

    41" x 27" $103

Roosevelt's Romance, *New York Sunday World*, ca. 1900, repaired, 17" x 22"   . . .$230

Skyride, 1933, World's Fair attraction, Art Deco style, 24" x 16" $1,265

Son of Frankenstein, ca. 1930s, movie poster $7,500

Super Black Champions, Caribbean Communications, ca. 1970s, Ali, Johnson,

    Robinson, etc., matted, 9 1/2" x 12" $287

Thurston's Vanishing Whippet automobile, 1928   . . . .$880

U.S.A. Bonds, with Boy Scout, 1918, J.C. Leyendecker, repaired, 30" x 20"   . . . $258

Wallace Bros. Circus, ca. 1950s, 28" x 41" $125

Whoopee Party, 1932, Walt Disney's Mickey Mouse, 27" x 41" $4,500

Yes Sir I Am Here, Recruits Wanted, 1918, Edward Penfield, 39" x 26 1/2",

    Carey Print Litho. $3,450

Your New Year, 1929, Mather and Company work incentive poster depicting children,

    43 1/2" x 35" $750

chapter twelve
advertising signs

Over the past century or so, advertising signs could be found outside or inside. They might be proclaiming a new product or simply attracting customers to an already established one. Some signs provided information, or even warnings, but nearly all had some commercial connection or at least the hint of something for sale.

They differed from traditional advertising posters in that they usually were much more durable (typically a fairly heavy cardboard), and were normally far less dependent on time as a significant factor in their message. More often than not it was bright colors and striking images of children, animals, or the products themselves that attracted the attention of the passer-by.

Starting with the last quarter of the nineteenth century, advertising signs had different names and even slightly different uses. They were known as banners, counter cards, hangers, placards, store cards, site-of-sale cards, and various other titles. They could vary in size from six or eight inches to several feet. The one thing most of them had in common was the same narrow purpose of attention attracting advertising. They were not sold, nor were they given away as a premium (unlike their kid sister trade cards). The fact is, they were nearly always thrown away to make room for other advertising signs. Nearly always, but not always.

Early site of sale sign, thin cardboard, full-color lithograph, ca. 1880s.

Back in the 1880s, an obscure folk artist living in the Midwest would visit stores near his home and obtain advertising signs shopkeepers had discarded. The artist was not as interested in the signs' messages as he was in their perfectly clear reverse sides. The blank backs made great sketch boards for the artist, who would make detailed renderings of wood carvings and iron moldings before taking the delicate work a step further. The carvings of the folk artist became fairly well-known in the region. The sketches were forgotten, however, until they were uncovered by descendants nearly 100 years later in a carefully wrapped, large-sized album. The pencil drawings of that nineteenth-century artist were not impressive, but the collection of brightly colored lithographed signs that served as sketch boards were wonderfully preserved.

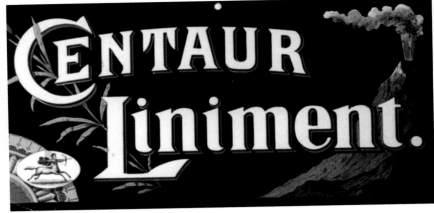

A full-color, nineteenth-century store sign for Centaur Liniment, ca. 1880s.

Early store sign, white on red, 12" x 12", ca. 1880s.

Right: Site of sale sign for Crescent pliers, ca. 1920s, 8" x 10", multi-colored, cardboard.

Piedmont tobacco advertising sign, ca. 1910, in three sections. Promotes cards, including Honus Wagner tobacco card, 60" x 40". (Leland's auction photo)

Right: Unusual highway-style sign, yellow and black, cardboard, promoting the 1987 film.

Left: Site of sale sign for a newspaper, three colors, 1990, 17" x 11".

Tobacco cardboard advertising sign, Christy Mathewson, 24" x 32", ca. 1914. (Leland's auction photo)

During the 1870s and 1880s, natural leaders in the medium of advertising on paper were the companies which sold patent medicines. For one thing, people generally tended to do their own doctoring in those days, particularly in the more isolated villages and towns. Thus, store-bought medications, even if they were openly advocated as "cure" for both man and animal, were eagerly sought. Not surprisingly, patent-medicine was highly profitable in the latter nineteenth century, with margins of return often in the 80 or 90 percent range for a bottle of cheaply made liniment. This combination of factors made patent medicine store signs very popular in American stores.

Would-be customers also saw a growing number of other products on advertising signs—soap, sugar, tobacco, firearms, and whiskey. Moreover, signs offered a wide assortment of other attractions, from hardware supplies to railroad transportation. For those who could read, and, perhaps even more importantly, for those who could only understand drawings and symbols, brand names began to take on major significance, from Baker's Chocolate, and Colgate, to Waterman's Pens and Winchester Arms. By the 1880s, a handful of leading companies were spending as much as $100,000 annually on paper advertising around the country.

Local stores held stocks of Centaur Liniment or Merchant's Gargling Oil with attractive advertising signs to alert customers. Advertising cards for Merchant's Gargling Oil proclaimed it as "a liniment for man and beast," with colorful images of healthy-looking horses. Fairbanks, Morse and Company offered both standard scales and windmills on its colorful signs, while store signs for E.F. Bradford's Leather and Rubber Hose and Belting were finely lettered and etched in two colors. Other signs promoted the J. M & I. Railroad, or even a traveling stage show.

Cardboard, multicolored store sign, ca. 1920s, Brinly Plows, 12" x 24".

Store advertising card for First Aid orange drink, ca. 1930s.

Wet Paint cardboard sign promoting Carter White Lead paint, ca. 1920s.

Multicolored store sign, ca. 1930s, for Rem cough medication.
Artwork by Lucian Bernhard.

Looney Tunes movie standee, ca. 1936, multicolored.

Store display for Pal Razor blades, ca. 1950s.

Store sign in full color, Rayette hair care products, ca. 1960s, 26" x 22".

158 advertising signs

Site-of-sale sign, black and white, nurse image with Kotex package, ca. 1950s.

Seven-Up site of sale sign, 25" x 18 1/2", ca. 1950s.

Seven-Up point of purchase sign with Santa, dated 1955. Height 21".

Old Crown Ale/Beer sign, 12" x 17", full color, ca. 1960s.

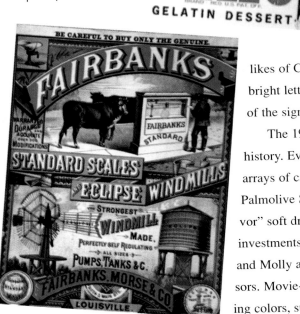

Early in the twentieth century, advertising signs and more elaborate display signs began to play a larger role in retailing. The advances of lithographed printing added to the color and attractiveness of such signs as they did with other printed advertising. Around 1910, the Piedmont Company issued a stunning three-sided "crowd in the ball park" display sign promoting cigarettes and the interesting little baseball cards that came with them. The 60" x 40" display illustrated the cards of ten different players, including Honus Wagner. It was the Wagner card that later became one of those most sought after baseball cards of the twentieth century. The Piedmont display has become a sought after item as well. In recent years, a rare example brought more than $3,000 at Leland's leading sports memorabilia auction in New York City.

Leland's has also sold other treasured baseball-related advertising signs such as Tuxedo's colorful depiction of player great Christy Mathewson, issued around 1914, and a 16" diameter die-cut ad sign used a few years later by Reach Baseball Equipment, which provided the official baseball at that time for the American League.

Retail stores in the 1920s offered advertising signs for the likes of Crescent pliers and Brinly Plows. Manufacturers made use of bright letters on lightly colored but heavy cardboard stock for a majority of the signs.

The 1930s saw the greatest assortment of advertising signs thus far in history. Even the most bland of retail and grocery stores offered dazzling arrays of cardboard symbols, from Donald Duck Butter Creams candy and Palmolive Soap to Dutch Boy Paint and First Aid, the "orange fruity flavor" soft drink. Entertainment also became a factor in advertising sign investments with radio shows like Tom Mix, Chandu, and Fibber McGee and Molly appearing in cardboard form along with their radio show sponsors. Movie-goers, meanwhile, were treated to advertising standees in blazing colors, such as Looney Tunes cartoons, in the lobby of theaters. In some cases, the artwork of well-known commercial artists, such as Lucian Bernard for Rem cough medication, was added to the growing parade of colorful advertising signs.

Up-Town soft drink store sign, full color, ca. 1960s. 18" x 13 1/2", Toledo, Ohio.

JELL-O ad featuring Mickey Mantle, 1962, color, 34" x 28".(Leland's auction photo)

Highly colorful 1880s store sign from Fairbanks, Morse and Co., 9" x 12".

During the war years of the 1940s, many ad signs were devoted to bond sales and "war loan" causes. Frequently, they were gaily decorated in patriotic colors and slogans. Meanwhile, school children were depicted in various signs, including those for GE Mazda electric light bulbs. Animated characters also made more and more appearances on cardboard for commercial firms: the Kool Penguin for Kool Cigarettes, and Elsie the Cow for Borden dairy products. In the 1950s, there were character connections with television show sponsors, such as Colgate Dental Cream with Howdy Doody. Another star-related sign promoted Ball Brand Summerettes footwear with a photo of Lucille Ball and a mention of her latest movie, *Sorrowful Jones*. Additionally, soft drink producers like Coca-Cola and Seven-Up used a number of full-color cardboard signs to link their product with the simple joys of pie, ice cream, grilled cheese, or a hamburger. Green Spot Orange Drink used healthy and happy children on their product signs.

Topics for advertising in the 1960s extended to Sealtest Ice Cream, Piels Beer, Old Crown Ale, Up-Town soft drinks, and Rayette professional hair care. In 1962, JELL-O featured baseball legend Mickey Mantle on a site-of-sale sign promoting its product and accompanying trading cards. In the mid-1990s one such surviving sign sold at Leland's memorabilia auction for more than $225.

Die-cut adv. sign, cardboard. Reach Official American League baseball, 16" diameter, 1920s. (Leland's auction photo)

In recent years presidential candidate Jimmy Carter has appeared on a store sign promoting *Playboy* magazine and his famous interview with that publication, and no less than the Three Stooges themselves clowned from grocery store signs on behalf of Hostess bakery products.

The good news for collectors and would-be collectors is that colorful advertising signs are still, after more than a century, very much in use. They range from Kellogg's Corn Flakes in the grocery aisles to the daily newspaper on brightly painted vending machines. The author's own office is decorated with a smashing six-foot standee put out for the Halloween season a few years ago by Hershey's. Complete with ghost, pumpkin and black cat, it never fails to draw the attention of visitors (especially those age seven and under.)

Cardboard cutout sign for the Coca-Cola Company, featuring a bathing suit girl, 1926. Full color, 18" x 22".

Ball Brand Summerettes footwear, features Lucille Ball, countertop display, some wear, 12" x 17", ca. 1950 . . . . $220

Beechnut Chewing Tobacco, Jack Dempsey vs. Gene Tunney, "the Scrap of the Century," cardboard display sign, 38" x 60", 1928, minor restoration $2,009

Borden dairy products, Elsie the Cow, full color, die-cut cardboard, 15" x 20", ca. 1940s, some repair $120

E.F. Bradford and Co., leather and rubber hose and belting, ca. 1880s, 12" x 12", red and white lettering $52

Brinly Plows, green and red, ca. 1920s, 12" x 24" $45

Carter White Lead Paint, "wet paint" cardboard sign, red on white cardboard, ca. 1920s $5

Centaur Liniment, full color, ca. 1880s, near mint, striking lithograph, heavy cardboard $32

Chesterfield Cigarettes, Lou Durocher and Casey Stengel, "New York Champions," 1951, full-color cardboard sign, 22" x 21" $2,440

Chesterfield Cigarettes, Top Men in America's Sports, cardboard sign, full color, includes Joe DiMaggio and Ben Hogan, ca. 1950s, 14" x 23" $680

Chicago Tribune, Indy Action race car, red, white, and blue vendor sign, 1990 . . . . $5

Coca-Cola, umbrella and woman in bathing suit, 1926, 18" x 22", full color . . .$1,500

Crescent pliers, ca. 1920s, 8" x 10" cardboard, multicolored $35

Fairbanks, Morse & Co., standard scales and windmills, striking lithograph, ca. 1880s, 9" x 12" $60

Farmers Mutuals Insurance, No Smoking Please, red and blue on white cardboard, ca. 1950s $12

First Aid orange-flavored fruit drink, red and purple on white cardboard, ca. 1930s $12

G.E. Mazda light bulbs, die-cut cardboard schoolchild holding bulb, 13" x 24", ca. 1940s, some wear $60

Goldsmith Athletic Goods, baseballs, "First Because They Last," cardboard sign, 13" x 14", full color, ca. 1920s $770

Granger Tobacco, baseball star Johnny Mize, full-color cardboard, 14" x 20", ca. 1950s $330

Green Spot Orange Drink, die-cut cardboard with waxed carton, full color, 12" x 17", ca. 1950s $55

J. M & I. railroad line, trolley card, ca. 1890s, blue, pink, and white $25

Jell-o, Mickey Mantle and trading cards, 34" x 28", full color $325

Johnson's Wax, Fibber McGee and Molly countertop standee, die-cut cardboard, 18" x 14", promotes radio show, some repair, 1937 . . . .$120

Kellogg's, promotes contest, features Tucan Sam, Apple Jacks Kids, Dig 'Em Frog and others, two-sides, full color, 11" x 29", 1982 . . . .$24

Kotex, nurse holding regular box, black and white, ca. 1950s, considerable
wear and aging $8

Looney Tunes, movie standee, ca. 1936, multicolored $525

Lucky Strike Cigarettes, baseball star Waite Hoyt, 22", oval, ca. 1950s $330

Lucky Strike Cigarettes, baseball star Tony Lazzeri, cardboard trolley sign,
full color, 1927, 21" x 12" $1,420

Merchant's Gargling Oil, ca. 1880s, for man and beast, brittle edges and
crumbling, full color $38

Old Crown Ale, Irish Water Spaniel in simulated wood frame, 12" x 17",
ca. 1960s $42

Old Gold Cigarettes, football player Red Grange-look alike, standee, full-color
cardboard, 31" x 41", ca. 1930s $550

Pal safety razor blades, colorful dispensing display complete with 12 packages,
ca. 1950s $40

Piedmont cigarettes, three sections promoting baseball cards including Honus
Wagner, ca. 1910, full color, 60" x 40" $3,200

P.F. Canvas Shoes, Big League Baseball Stars, includes Mickey Mantle and Stan
Musial, cardboard sign, full color, ca. 1950s, 24" x 16" $990

P.F. Canvas Shoes, star baseball player Warren Saphn, full-color cardboard sign,
12" x 16", ca. 1950s $360

Pinch Hit Tobacco, baseball player "hit of the day," full-color cardboard, 60" x 30"
early 1920s, framed $750

Playboy magazine with black and white photo of Jimmy Carter, 1976
presidential campaign $25

Post Cereal, Hopalong Cassidy Trading Cards, full-color cardboard, 13" x 26",
ca. 1950, mounted on white paper backing $1,250

Raising Arizona movie promotion, highway-style sign, 1987, yellow cardboard
with black lettering $4

Rayette professional hair care, stylish woman, full color, 26" x 22", ca. 1960s $18

Rawlings sporting goods, Mickey Mantle in uniform with glove, full-color
cardboard, ca. 1950s, near mint condition, 24" x 21" $4,600

Reach sports equipment, Official American League Baseball, die-cut color, 16"
diameter sign, ca. 1920s $350

Rem cough medication, ca. 1930s, artist Lucian Bernhard, multicolored $50

Servais Le Roy and Flying Visit magic act, ca. 1890s, window card, lithographed
by Weller of London $305

Seven-Up 'fresh up here,' site of sale, red, white, green, 25" x 18 1/2" ca. 1950s .. $42

Seven-up, Santa with holiday wreath, 1955, 21", full color $44

Tuxedo tobacco, baseball star Christy Mathewson in stunning lithographed color,
24" x 32", ca. 1914 ....$5,000

Up-Town soft drink, 1960s, Uptown Beverage Co. 18" x 14", Toledo,
Ohio, multicolored $32

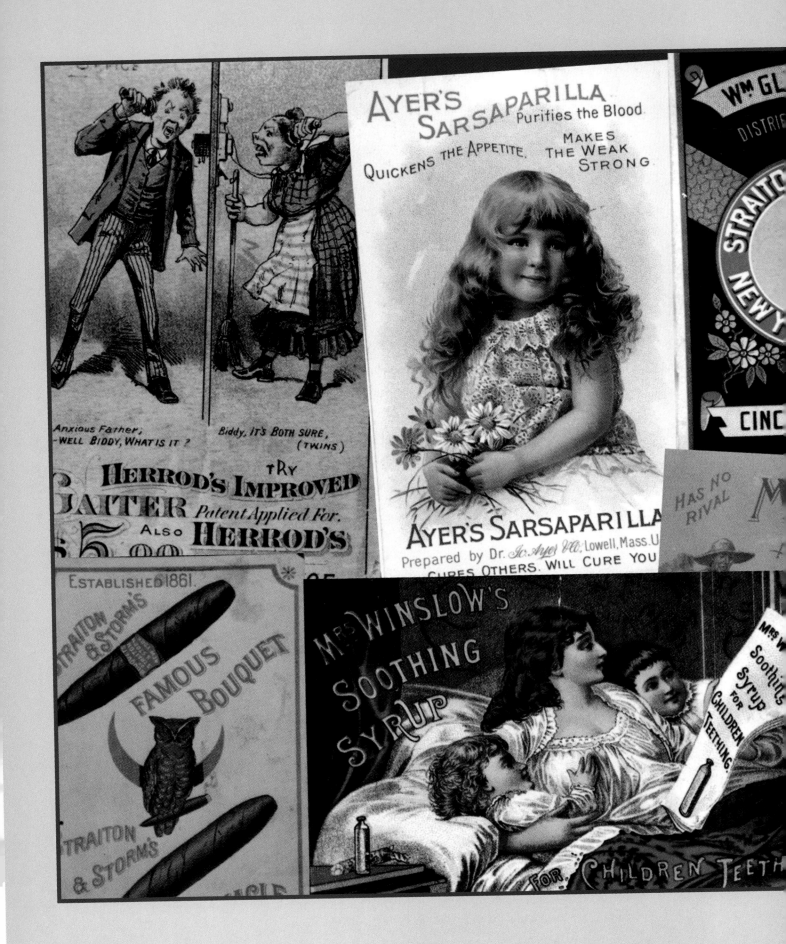

chapter thirteen
advertising trade cards

Trade cards in the nineteenth century became, nearly at once, charming, colorful, controversial, and quite collectible.

In a sense, they were the last step in the evolution of direct advertising from the merchant. In colonial days, shop keepers depended mainly on signs hung from above their doors. Since most customers of the era could not read, a cigar store Indian identified the tobacco store; a one-dimensional shoe, the shoe repair; a giant tooth, the dentist, and so forth.

During the late eighteenth century, a certain number of business cards were issued by leading bootmakers, cabinetmakers, silversmiths, and others. They were printed from engravings and sometimes woodcuts; some even had fancy borders around them. Typically, these cards offered only the basic information from the merchant, printed on light cardboard or coarse paper, and were distributed in hopes they would be kept by customers for future reference.

London trade card from 1788 advertising ladies foundation garments. Similar to trade signs.

"Since our ancestors were not given to wasting paper, they often saved (early) trade cards for no other reason than to cipher and make notes on the backs," observed author Morgan Towne in the 1949 book, *Treasures in Truck & Trash*. Towne told of purchasing several cards dating from the 1760s which were being used nearly a century later for notations like, "March 11, 1859, set the blue hen today and broke ground for onion setts."

Many years ago, collectors set about to gather the older basic business cards, especially those of the more famous cabinetmakers and other tradesmen. Even in the 1940s and 1950s there was talk of finding an authentic card from legendary silversmith and patriot Paul Revere; however, the true trade cards of dazzling color, while they undoubtedly drew their names from the colorless cards distributed by eighteenth century tradesmen, would come much later in the evolution.

By the middle of the nineteenth century, embossing and even a bit of color was being added to business cards, and there was enough interest for printers to provide the service for other merchants.

In 1855, a newspaper advertisement appeared on behalf of E. Ketterlinus of Philadelphia:

Colorful trading card for Herrod's Gaiter Shoes, late nineteenth century.

"We invite the attention of Dealers and others to our splendid stock of embossed Show cards, Perfumery, Fabric, Wine and Liquor Labels, the largest and most varied assortment in the United States. Jar and Drawer labels printed in Gold Leaf and Bronze. Lettering navy, gold, bronze, green; framed in gray, red, gold; ornate design."

One of the greatest users of newly emerging trade cards in the 1850s were owners of clipper ships. The ships would take passengers and freight to specific ports in record times and, for a time, were quite the transportation rage. Just one year after the Ketterlinus ad, William Nesbit of New York issued a catalog of 48 different clipper ship cards, each printed in full color.

Like the earlier merchant's business cards, the clipper ship trade cards with their hundreds of different designs were grabbed up by collectors during the first half of the twentieth century, and are relatively scarce today.

During the 1870s, two major developments merged to give America what would henceforth be known as the "true" advertising trade card. One was the breakthrough in chromolithographic printing which provided amazing color with relative ease. Another was the country's first real need for national advertising. With the transcontinental railroad having been completed in 1869, the American marketplace loomed from coast to coast.

Moreover, products of all sorts could be moved from coast to coast and all the stops in-between.

The trade card then, like nothing before or since, represented the tremendous consumer transition from simple posted notices to full-sized, full-color advertisements. It was also a transition from basic black-and-white printing to technologically advanced color in commercial messages.

One of the first major appearances of large numbers of varied advertising trade cards took place at the 1876 Centennial Exposition in Philadelphia. Written accounts say vast numbers were distributed by individual businesses and manufacturers to countless visitors who, in turn, carried them back home to American cities and towns. National publishers like Louis Prang and Company, Julius Bien Company, and Currier and Ives soon mastered the lithographic color process, and eventually it was adapted by regional and local printing companies.

Other circumstances also favored the blossoming of trade cards. Such cards would make perfect premiums for manufacturers who were doing away with barrels, burlap sacks, and bulk containers in general for smaller, more distinctive and recognizable

Ayer's Hair Vigor, mermaids and sailing ship, ca. 1880s.

labeled packages. The cards (often with the image of the product clearly reproduced on them) could be inserted in the packages or given away at the counter in retail stores which sold the national product.

Besides specific national product cards, merchants could also use stock trade cards as giveaway premiums and for store promotional purposes. These cards were typically provided by local printers and were designed for the imprint of most any store or service. With either of these card types, the merchant could add the name and address of his business merely with a handstamp if necessary.

At the same time, the cards were also perfect for the growing consumer public which, until then, had little access to reading material beyond a few books, a farming almanac, and the family Bible. Adding illustrations in color simply made these trendy new trade cards all the more unique and irresistible.

Naturally, people around America began collecting them. Postage stamps not withstanding, "there is every evidence, that these cards were one of the first paper collectibles to be acquired and assembled in an organized manner," according to the book, *Paper Collectibles, The Essential Buyer's Guide* (Wallace-Homestead). Some collected the trade cards and stored them in boxes under their bed, while others pasted them in elaborate books and proudly displayed them in their Victorian parlor. Collecting the cards was such a wide-spread pastime that albums especially made for preserving them were offered in leading stores and in mail-order catalogs.

Gen. Grant on tobacco advertising card, ca. 1872-1876. (Hake's Americana, York, PA)

Household Sewing Machine Company trade card, from the 1880s, depicting woman and child; full color.

Right: Straiton & Storm's cigars, with owl symbol, on an 1887 trade card.

Reed & Carnick powdered milk product trade card, from the 1890s.

"The Champion," Belding Bros. Co. trade card, ca. 1890s.

Winslow's Soothing Syrup patent medicine trade card, ca. 1890s.

Scenic view trade card, Willimantic cotton thread, ca. 1890s.

Scott's Emulsion "Twins" patent medicine trade card, ca. 1890s.

Lovely little girl on Ayer's Sarsaparilla trade card; full color.

Many companies, aware of the rising collectibility of such cards, issued them in sets; thus, encouraging customers to return to the same store for the same product to complete entire sets. Sometimes as many as 50 or more cards were a part of a single series. Tobacco and cigarette makers often favored birds, entertainers, military leaders, and even sports figures for their series. Pretty young women, children and animals were most often illustrated on the cards of other manufacturers. Frequently, the children were engaged in playful scenes or playfully riding on carts, wagons, or even on roller skates. Patriotic themes were also popular, along with those showing people happily at work. An exception to most standards was an 1880s card for Ayer's Hair Vigor. It depicted scantily clad mermaids in its theme—considered quite daring for the Victorian period.

Certainly, the many trade cards produced varied in size, but, for the most part, they were two or three inches wide and four or five inches deep—just right for pocket, purse, or for inserting into small packages.

"The cards did more than just carry a commercial message," noted Jack Golden in the Time-Life *Encyclopedia of Collectibles* of the 1970s. "They gave beguiling glimpses of the good life, supplied innocent amusement and provided useful advice—on some cards, for example, housewives were offered instructions for washing clothes and cooking meals." Among the biggest users of trade card advertising during the late nineteenth century were producers of stoves, soaps, patent medicines, farm equipment, tobacco, and sewing supplies. A vast majority represented things which were customarily sold directly to, and used by, housewives themselves.

At the height of the trade card popularity near the close of the nineteenth century, nearly every store and shop in the country found one of three ways to distribute the cards to the public:

1. Product cards were generously provided by national manufacturers and could be handed out at stores, or even mailed to good customers.

2. Stock cards had nice designs but promoted no particular product. Sometimes the local dealer's name and

Sewing machine trade card, Lozier & Stokes, copyright 1882.

address was printed or simply hand-stamped on them. These, too, could be given directly to customers.

3. Insert-cards promoted the product and often served as an in-the-package premium. Typically, they were numbered and issued in sets of varying numbers. Of course, the issuance of trade cards was so extensive and diverse that any combination of the above categories could be used as well.

Besides the standard but highly colorful trade card, there were a number of more elaborate issues. Among them were die-cut cards which were printed in the shape of a specific object, such as an apple or acorn. There were also metamorphic cards, which could be folded to create a different scene or a different face on the card. A good example of a metamorphic card is one issued in the 1870s by Blackwell's (Bull) Durham tobacco. One view of the card depicted President U.S. Grant—flipped over, it presented the image of presidential candidate Samuel Tilden.

In addition, there were see-through cards, which enhanced the image when held to the light much like some postcards of a somewhat later era. There were also puzzle view cards which presented an image within an image. In the 1880s, Phenyo-Caffeine Company issued a card for their "headache cures" brand with an apparent young girl. Readers were asked to find her mother within the same black and white drawing. Probably least issued, because of the added expense involved, were mechanical trade cards—which offered some hand-moveable part. Most all of the trade cards with "extras" are more highly prized by collectors than a standard card from a comparable advertiser. Mechanical cards, fewer in number and subject to damage, probably top the list of all trade cards.

Puzzle view trade card for Phenyo-Caffeine Co., 1880s, with girl and her mother. (Skinner Inc. auction photo)

Like so many other antiques and collectibles, trade card collecting appears to have happened in cycles. After being highly popular at the turn of the century, public interest waned. In the 1930s, Morgan Towne wrote that a mere ten years earlier, albums pasted full of trade cards sold for a dollar each—now they go for five to $50 dollars. Towne estimated that in 1949 there were only 25,000 collectors of chrome-lithographed cards, and most of them collected by subject, such as birds, animals, or wheeled vehicles—much as they had during the onset of such cards.

For further reading:

Victorian Trade Cards, by Dave Cheadle (Collector Books)

Frogs were dressed as sailors for Durham Tobacco in this 1880s trade card.

Buckeye Lawn Mower
trade card, 1880s. Mast,
Foos, & Co.

Dr. Radliffes Great Remedy trade card seeking
"Good agents," ca. 1880s.

B.T. Babbitt's Best Soap trade card, 1880s;
full color.

Street scene trade card, Rapid Transit Soap, from Colgate & Co., 1880s.

Blacks depicted on Durham Smoking Tobacco on trade card, 1880s.

Agents for Straiton & Storm's New York Cigars, 1886; full color.

J & P Coats cotton thread trade card, ca. 1880s; full color.

David's Prize Soap trade card, 1876; full color.

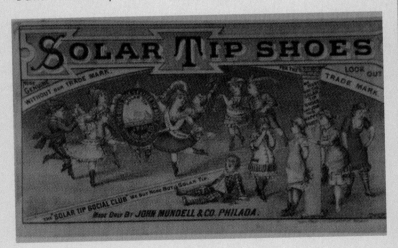

Solar Tip Shoes trade card, ca. 1890s.

Trade card for Mica Axle Grease, with horse and wagon, ca. 1890.

Ayer's Hair Vigor, mermaids and sailing ship, 1880s $12

Ayer's Sarsaparilla, girl with flowers, ca. 1890s $9

B.T. Babbitt's Best Baking Powder, boy on soap box, 1880s $14

Belding Bros. Co. "Champion" thread, girl on skates, ca. 1890s $8

Berry Bros., Uncle Sam and cans of varnish, late nineteenth century $20

Buckeye Lawn Mower, woman mowing grass, Mast, Foos, & Co., 1880s $22

Ceresota, copyright 1902, Queen and Knave of Hearts, The Gray Lith. Co. $16

Chase & Sanborn coffee, full color, copyright 1886, Forbes Co. $10

David's Prize Soap, children and dog cart, patent 1876 . . . .$13

Drink Hires Root Beer/Put Roses in Your Cheeks, full color, ca. 1891 . . . . $18

Durham Tobacco, frogs dressed as sailors, 1880s $20

Durham Smoking Tobacco, two black couples, "pairs of twins," 1880s $30

Empire Wringer Co., ca. 1890s, young girl demonstrates wringer $25

Ferndell Coffee with Buster Brown, full color, front lifts up, copyright 1903,
    Kaufmann & Strauss Co. $30

Herrod's Gaiter Shoes, comic characters on telephone, copyright 1883 . . . .$11

Hood's Pills, full color die-cut, Cure Liver Ills, young girl $10

Household Sewing Machine Company, sewing woman and child, 1880s $14

J & P Coats cotton thread, boy aboard train, ca. 1880s $10

Kumysgen powdered milk, man milking cow, Reed & Carnrick, 1890s $12

Lion Coffee, ca. 1894, full color, boy and puppy $6

Lydia Pinkham, ca. 1880s, Yours For Health, Pinkham portrait $14

Mica Axle Grease, horse and wagon, ca. 1890s $16

New Home Sewing Machine, boy with horn, Lozier & Stokes dealers,
    copyright 1882 . . . .$10

National Surgical Institute, ca. 1890s, boy on crutches, slightly trimmed $35

The Oval Churn, horizontal card, ca. 1890s, production factory on reverse,
    creasing and wear $20

Phenyo-Caffeine Co. 1880s Puzzel View black & white $20

Dr. Radcliffe's Great Remedy for "all aches and pains," lengthy text on reverse . .$30

Rapid Transit Soap, street scene, 1880s, Colgate & Co. $22

Red Cross Base Burner stove, ca. 1880s, ornate examples of stoves $12

Scott's Emulsion "Twins" girls promote patent medicine, ca. 1890s $16

Solar Tip Shoes, dancing characters, ca. 1890s, ...$15

Straiton & Storm's New York Cigars, 1886, with owl, Glenn & Sons $12

Straiton & Storm's cigars, with owl, 1887 . . . .$10

Willimantic Thread, bridge scene includes balloon, ca. 1890s $18

Mrs. Winslow's Soothing Syrup, mother and children, patent medicine, ca. 1890s .$16

chapter fourteen

everything else that is paper advertising

Fairly early in my youth, the financial bread and butter of my life were handbills. I was not buying or selling them, of course, just passing them out in neighborhoods and on street corners. During the late 1940s and early 1950s, handbills were still a pretty good means of advertising for merchants in small towns who had little other means, or for merchants in large towns who couldn't afford, or didn't need, the greater distribution of newspapers. During the week, there were handbills for auctions, dry cleaners, and retail stores. On Saturday mornings came the handbills for the local movie theater, where Westerns were the usual fare. Handbills featuring the current Six Gun stars, among other attractions, were slipped under the wipers of every windshield on the courthouse square and left in every barber shop and grocery. The going rate for the unskilled distributing of most stacks of handbills was usually 50 cents or so, but the Saturday matinee handbills were worth that, plus two free passes to the likes of Gene Autry and Champion in *Mule Train*. Wow!

Handbill promoting a Gene Autry Western movie, 1940s.

Handbills, though, certainly were not and are not the only paper advertising to be gathered under the listing of "everything else." There are scores of selections that may not be major categories—yet—but that are drawing increased attention as additional ways of collecting commercial images of the past. They range from advertising manuals to soap wrappers, and reach from sports scorecards and schedules to bookmarks and bottle toppers.

The following are a number of specific categories which offer significant material to the collector.

BOOKLETS, BROCHURES, PAMPHLETS, AND FLYERS

Here is a rapidly growing area with roots in the early twentieth century. Early in the

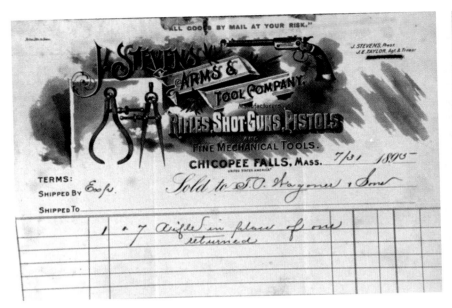

J. Stevens Arms & Tool Co. billhead for a rifle replacement, dated 1895.

Advertising booklet issued to smokers by P. Lorillard, 1882.

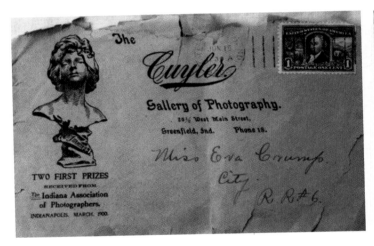

Advertising envelope for "Gallery of Photography," used in direct mailing, 1904.

Broom label, early twentieth century, Amsterdam Broom Company, 3 1/4" x 4 3/4".

Ivory Soap wrapper, early 1900s, with 13-star Man-in-Moon trademark; blue & white.

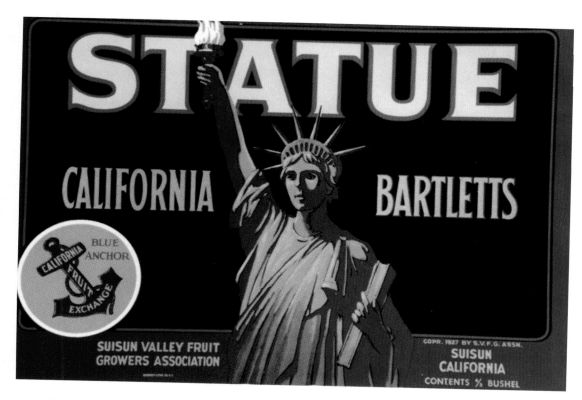

Statue fruit crate label from California, 1927.

Advertising booklet with sewing kit, for Hygeia Coffee, 1925.

Dilling's Marshmallows advertising recipe booklet, ca. 1920s, pocket-sized.

Wilbur's Cocoa, container-shaped booklet, ca. 1930s and Maud Tousey Fangel, artist.

1900s, prospering firms provided booklets with basic information, and often with space for record keeping to loyal customers. Their firm was usually well-represented on the colorful covers, and sometimes the advertising extended to inside pages—but other space inside often allowed for personal jottings. Places like A. Hoff, in Mount Horeb, Wisconsin, or Schnull Groceries, in Indianapolis, Indiana, felt customers who kept careful records would soon realize the savings in dealing with these merchants.

For much of the twentieth century, brochures and flyers with sparkling colors were freely distributed to encourage customers to purchase, travel, enjoy, invest, or even be careful. During the 1950s, some of the most attractive and colorful brochures came from the Federal Civil Defense Administration, describing the threat of nuclear attack.

A. Hoff store advertising booklet for records, early 1900s, pocket-sized.

BOXES AND CONTAINERS

For decades, beautifully designed product boxes and containers were discarded after customer use. Tin or wood containers may have been spared for other uses, but paper and cardboard simply lacked the durability to be worth saving. Now, such boxes and containers are becoming collectibles. Wheaties boxes bearing baseball stars' images have been distinguished in the marketplace for some time. Then came the appeal of "kiddie" cereal boxes bearing big smiles for Tony the Tiger, the Sugar Bears, and such.

Such box/container appreciation also grew with collectors in other areas. For years, devotees of trading cards seldom concerned themselves with the cardboard display boxes that held their treasures at the retail stores. Today, these colorful display boxes (which at this point are empty) are more and more a part of the hobby. Donald Duck Straws or Mother's Oats packages, no longer holding a product, are sought for their distinctive and decorative collectibility. In recent years, a rather humble Cracker Jack box was put on the auction block by a national deal-

Kellogg's cereal box, with Tony the Tiger promoting an Admiral TV set prize, 1957.

Donald Duck Sunshine Straws, ca. 1950s; Herz Manufacturing, New York City.

Post Sugar Crisp cereal box promoting Mighty Mouse TV game, 1958.

er. The familiar red, white, and blue waxed paper box was missing both end flaps and had tears and age browning. Despite that, the early 1900s box brought more than $50.

BILLHEADS, CHECKS, ENVELOPES, INVOICES, LETTERHEADS

All but the most famous companies with the most dazzling designs and logos are still available to the curious and resourceful collector. Mail order auction firms like Cohasco,

Wrigley Company of Chicago letterhead with firm's vast complex depicted, ca. 1920s.

Inc. (Postal 821, Yonkers, NY 10702) are known to offer large lots of such material ranging from architect suppliers to sewing machine manufacturers. From Adams Express Company to Wrigley's Chewing Gum, most of this material was tossed away as worthless during the past century as businesses sought more space, merged or disappeared, and, in recent decades, went to electronic means of keeping records. Familiar old companies are favored, as well as those with sweeping graphics from the 1880s through the 1930s and beyond. Here is a rare case when a number of old bills can be a welcomed sight.

Lastly, consider this "shaggy dog" story about one particular letterhead. In 1994, Swann Galleries conducted a major auction of the memorabilia of film legend Joan Crawford. Among all the fantastic material was one dog-related item: a typed letter from the El Rancho Rin Tin Tin Ranch. Not surprisingly, the letter did not rate a mention in the auction gallery's advance press release for the great sale. The Swann catalog itself did, however, mention the 1956 letter and its inked pawprints of both Rin Tin Tin I and Rin Tin Tin IV "both on amusing letterhead of El Rancho Rin Tin Tin." The presale estimate on the canine correspondence and collectible letterhead was $80 to $120. It eventually sold at the auction for a startling $1,093.

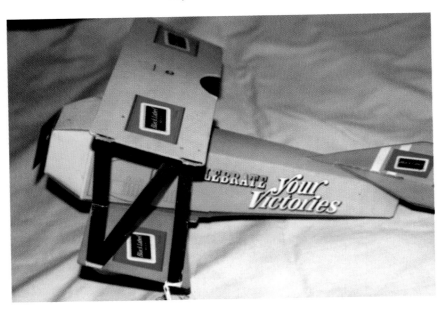

Black Label cardboard souvenir advertising airplane. Length 12", ca. 1950s.

CARDBOARD DISPLAYS AND SOUVENIRS

Here are striking items that were not quite signs and yet did not really fit into the reduced size of trade cards. These range from George Washington with a hatchet to a bi-winged plane promoting a once popular beer. Starting in the late nineteenth century, these clever cardboard or paper images in brightly printed colors helped sales locally and nationally. Chase and Sanborn used a cardboard coffee cup imprinted with their brand, while Atlantic and Pacific did something similar with a cardboard tea cup. Friend's Oats did a child in costume, and Gold Label Flour went with cardboard bunny rabbits. Magic Yeast offered a wise owl image, and Heinz produced their famous pickle in cardboard. Most of these displays and souvenir items didn't last long, but they were enormously popular while they did last. Not only did countertop displays qualify: Disney's great *Toy Story* was less than 18 months old when it was sold at a major auction house specializing in such enter-

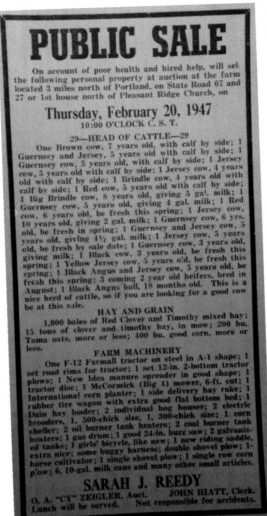

PUBLIC SALE

On account of poor health and hired help, will sell the following personal property at auction at the farm located 3 miles north of Portland, on State Road 67 and 27 or 1st house north of Pleasant Ridge Church, on

Thursday, February 20, 1947

10:00 O'CLOCK C. S. T.

29—HEAD OF CATTLE—29

One Brown cow, 7 years old, with calf by side; 1 Guernsey and Jersey, 5 years old, with calf by side; 1 Guernsey cow, 5 years old, with calf by side; 1 Jersey cow, 5 years old with calf by side; 1 Jersey cow, 4 years old with calf by side; 1 Brindle cow, 4 years old with calf by side; 1 Red cow, 5 years old with calf by side; 1 Big Brindle cow, 8 years old, giving 5 gal. milk; 1 Red Guernsey cow, 5 years old, giving 4 gal. milk; 1 Red cow, 6 years old, be fresh this spring; 1 Jersey cow, 10 years old, giving 2 gal. milk; 1 Guernsey cow, 6 yrs. old, be fresh in spring; 1 Guernsey and Jersey cow, 5 years old, giving 4½ gal. milk; 1 Jersey cow, 5 years old, be fresh by sale date; 1 Guernsey cow, 3 years old, giving milk; 1 Black cow, 3 years old, be fresh this spring; 1 Yellow Jersey cow, 5 years old, be fresh this spring; 1 Black Angus and Jersey cow, 5 years old, be fresh this spring; 3 coming 2 year old heifers, bred in August; 1 Black Angus bull, 18 months old. This is a nice herd of cattle, so if you are looking for a good cow be at this sale.

HAY AND GRAIN

1,000 bales of Red Clover and Timothy mixed hay; 15 tons of clover and timothy hay, in mow; 200 bu. Tama oats, more or less; 100 bu. good corn, more or less.

FARM MACHINERY

One F-12 Farmall tractor on steel in A-1 shape; 1 set road rims for tractor; 1 set 12-in. 2-bottom tractor plows; 1 New Idea manure spreader in good shape; 1 tractor disc; 1 McCormick (Big 1) mower, 6-ft. cut; 1 International corn planter; 1 side delivery hay rake; 1 rubber tire wagon with extra good flat bottom bed; 1 Dain hay loader; 2 individual hog houses; 2 electric brooders, 1, 500-chick size, 1, 300-chick size; 1 corn sheller; 2 oil burner tank heaters; 2 coal burner tank heaters; 1 gas drum; 1 good 24-in. buzz saw; 2 galvanized tanks; 1 girls' bicycle, like new; 1 new riding saddle, extra nice; some buggy harness; double shovel plow; 1 single shovel plow; 1 single row corn horse cultivator; 1 single shovel plow; 6, 10-gal. milk cans and many other small articles.

SARAH J. REEDY

O. A. "CY" ZEIGLER, Auct.   JOHN HIATT, Clerk.
Lunch will be served.   Not responsible for accidents.

Public sale handbill dated 1947, detailing a public auction, including cows, 10" x 5 1/2".

tainment material. The 10" x 12" cardboard display that offered a *Toy Story* backpack with the purchase of a CD-ROM, even with a small part missing, quickly sold for nearly $30.

HANDBILLS

Handbills have been used as a means of advertising for centuries, and have seldom been given the collector attention and appreciation they deserve. Handbills differed from posters by generally being smaller in size, and designed to be distributed in large quantities by hand. This meant they were often more cheaply prepared than posters, which would be printed in fewer numbers and "posted" to gather the attention of crowds. The handbill, meanwhile, was pressed into the waiting hand, dropped in the grocery sack, left in the seat of a vehicle, or shoved in the frame of a door.

Western movie handbills, mentioned in the introduction of this chapter, are good examples of handbills being held in little regard for many years. Theater owners in thousands of small and middle-sized towns used this form of advertising for years to promote their Saturday features which, of course, changed each week. Quite often, the film distributor provided the necessary art work for inexpensive copy work by the local printer. The final step was using youngsters (or adults) on Saturday mornings to distribute these handbills. Of course, they were almost never saved—unless a stack got shoved into the storeroom of the Main Street printer. Years later, a few wise collectors and Western fans figured out that if a sampling of these handbills had been saved each week in nearly any American town of the 1940s and 1950s, it would have produced what now would be a prized collection of Western film heroes.

Today, the general run of handbills, although relatively few in surviving numbers, are inexpensive and interesting. They offer an insight to life during earlier parts of the twentieth century—during the 1940s and 1950s, for example—when Frankfort Pilgrim College students did yard work and house cleaning for $1 per hour, and when full farms were sold at public auction "on account of poor health and hired help."

Handbills describing products which acquired later fame, and special events which

DRINK **Coca-Cola**

So easy to take home the six-bottle carton

Try It with Food—You'll Like It . . . .

Left: Coupon advertising card for six bottles of Coca-Cola from the late 1930s.

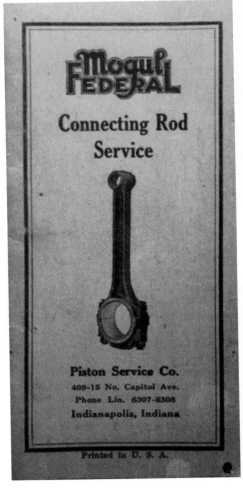

Mogul FEDERAL

Connecting Rod Service

Piston Service Co.
409-15 No. Capitol Ave.
Phone Lin. 6307-6308
Indianapolis, Indiana

Printed in U. S. A.

Mogul Federal Connecting Rod Service pocket-sized writing/record booklet, from 1934.

UNCLE SAM BRAND
YAKIMA VALLEY **Apples**
WAPATO FRUIT & COLD STORAGE CO.
WAPATO, WASH.
CONTENTS ONE BUSHEL BY VOLUME

Uncle Sam Brand Apples fruit label, from the Wapato Fruit & Cold Storage Co.

Right: Old Fashioned Mother's Oats, round cardboard container, full color.

COOKS IN 5 MINUTES

OLD FASHIONED **MOTHER'S OATS**

MINNESOTA HIGHWAY MAP 1935

Phillips 66

Phillips 66

Compliments of
Phillips Petroleum Company

ON RUSH BRAND
Melons
PRODUCE OF U.S.A
GROWN AND SHIPPED BY
Firebaugh, Calif. F. H. HOGUE CO. Yuma, Arizona ★ ★

On Rush Melons fruit crate label from Yuma, Arizona.

foods
MEN RAVE ABOUT
BY *Betty Crocker*

SERIES No. 4 · PRICE 15c

NOTE COUPON GOOD FOR *free* **SILVERWARE!**
1 VALUE COUPON ENCLOSED

BERLINER KRÄNZE

1½ cups shortening (use half butter for flavor)
1 cup sugar
Grated rind of one orange

2 eggs
4 cups GOLD MEDAL "Kitchen-tested" Flour

FOR MERINGUE
1 egg white

2 tbsp. sugar

METHOD—Cream the shortening, add sugar gradually, with the grated orange rind, and cream well. Beat eggs until light and add to the creamed mixture. Sift flour once before measuring. Stir in flour, mixing just enough to blend well. Chill dough for an hour. Break off small pieces and form into long rolls the length and size of pencils. Form a circle with each piece, bringing ends through in a single knot. Leave ½ inch end on each side. Make meringue by beating the egg white until stiff and adding the 2 tbsp. of sugar gradually. Brush tops of cookies with this meringue and bake on an ungreased cooky sheet. **Time—** Bake 10 to 15 minutes. **Temperature**—400° F., moderately hot oven. **Amount**—6 dozen. **Note**—These little wreaths may be trimmed just before placing in the oven, by sprinkling red and green decorettes on the center of the knot to look like a Christmas flower.

Phillips Petroleum Co. road map with airplane, 1935.

Betty Crocker advertising recipe pamphlet and coupon from 1935, 3 1/2" x 6 1/2".

proved to have some historic or social significance will, naturally, have value. Handbills from the nineteenth century are appreciated by today's collectors, particularly those that deal with patent medicines and other retail goods. Handbills promoting movie stars of the twentieth century are nearly always popular if in fairly good condition. Those promoting mega collectible products such as Coca-Cola, Campbell's Soup, pottery, glassware, and toys will command a premium because they strongly attract "crossover" collectors. Handbills were also used, to a limited extent, in various presidential campaigns around the United States.

LABELS AND BOOKMARKS

Labels, of course, have been around in this country since they were proudly presented by colonial cabinetmakers, and even before. Craftsmen who did not stamp their name on handmade products—from chairs to picture frames—often included printed labels. After the 1860s, every box of cigars sold in America was clearly labeled, and as the quality of printing rapidly improved, cigar labels and those of many other products became rainbows of dazzling color. As much as anything else, they were designed to catch the eye of the consumer who, until the 1870s, was much more used to rather bland-looking packages. Those who marketed produce in the late nineteenth century—and through the first third of the twentieth century—were equally enamored with the dashing display of lithographic colors. Their delightful labels helped sell everything from apples to yams for the better part of a half century. Attached paper labels on most products had generally become obsolete by the 1950s, when the selling image expanded to the entire package, and its full and faithful reproduction in print media.

Advertising on paper bookmarks did not enjoy the glamorous history of paper labels. This form of advertising was a standard practice, however, as early as the latter part of the nineteenth century. Advertisers who cast their lot with the more thoughtful "reading" consumers ranged from American

Advertising bookmark for tubes of Easy Dye, produced by American Color Co. in the 1890s; made of cardboard.

Color Company's Easy Dye to White Star Line Ocean Liners. During the busy twentieth century, advertising on bookmarks was, for the most part, more entertainment and social-cause related—with obvious promotions for books (and sometimes movies), along with messages from groups like the American Cancer Society. Today, paper advertising bookmarks remain relatively under-collected and, potentially, a very rewarding part of the overall collectibles field.

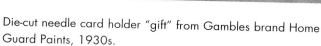

Die-cut needle card holder "gift" from Gambles brand Home Guard Paints, 1930s.

Farmers Fertilizer Co. advertising booklet of needles, ca. 1920s.

NEEDLE BOOKS

At one time, especially during the 1920s and 1930s, just about every major manufacturer in search of customers made an attempt with needle books. Most of them looked simply like booklets on the outside, bearing the company's message and often the image of the packaged product. Inside was a double-page assortment of needles. Even before the war years of the 1940s, they had grown too expensive to freely hand out to the general public. Moreover, sewing by hand as a household activity had also significantly declined. Today, they are interesting collectibles, almost always found in good condition at reasonable prices.

RECIPE, COUPON, AND COOKBOOKS

During the first half of the twentieth century, manufacturers of everything from baking powder to electric ranges believed that cooking instructions would enhance the sales of their products. The Royal Baking Powder Company's

JELL-O booklet from 1923 with a Maxfield Parrish cover: "Polly Put the Kettle On."

baker and pastry cookbook, with a brilliantly illustrated cover, was on the market by 1902 and, undoubtedly, added to the popularity of the product. Most such recipe or cooking booklets were given away or sold for a few cents. (One exception was the Federal Range operating instructions and cookbook which sold for $1, even in 1929.) Sometimes these items were included in the product's package; sometimes they were stacked as a display at the site of the product's sale; and, later, many were distributed through mail-order requests. Possibly the most famous of the paper advertising cook booklets were those produced in the 1920s and 1930s by JELL-O, using the talents of such well-known artists as Maxfield Parrish.

By the 1930s, competition was keen enough and times were economically tight enough that many companies turned to coupons. Betty Crocker, for example, combined a free silverware coupon with a recipe booklet in 1935. It was priced at 15 cents. Coca-Cola became one of the first soft drink firms to offer coupons in the 1930s. Just slightly smaller than postcards, these full-color cardboard coupons could be presented to neighborhood dealers for six bottles of Coke.

Cookbook and operating instructions by Federal Electric Range. Price was $1 in 1929.

ROAD MAPS

In the 1890s, the *Chicago Herald* produced a promotional and advertising road map specifically for cars rather than bicycles, and for the next 50 years commercial firms, especially oil and gasoline companies, flooded the motoring marketplace with them. By the 1920s, an automobile's glove compartment could be stuffed with commercially produced road maps from the likes of

Wadhams, winged-horse on a road map of Wisconsin, 1936.

Vacuum Oil Company, Gulf Gasoline, Bekins Moving and Storage, and Monarch Oil Refining.

Throughout the 1920s and 1930s, promotional road maps remained the simple, but strikingly colorful, single-page folding type freely given at most any gas station. In 1935, the Standard Oil Company published their 15th edition of such maps. Across the country, similar advertising-related maps were being produced and distributed by oil companies ranging from En-Ar-Col and Deep Rock, to Texas Pacific Coal and Oil and White Eagle Gasoline. Mobile Gas joined the leaders by handing out maps with their familiar "flying red horse" at more than 1,700 stations every year. The early 1940s were prosperous for oil companies, and they continued their massive road map promotions; however, the onset of World War II and the accompanying gas rationing put a major halt to auto travel for a great majority of Americans. Advertising road maps were still a major giveaway of the 1950s, although many lacked the zestful color and graphics of earlier issues. By the 1960s, the promotional types were pretty much gone, and motorists had little recourse but to "buy retail" from Rand McNally and others.

Until the 1990s, these wonderfully graphic road maps of the past were seldom collected at all. A major factor in the growth of their popularity was the growing number of collectors nationwide who longed for anything related to service stations and their many products. Moreover, people in other areas of collecting began to see the potential of displaying such promotional maps with grand names and images emblazed upon them. Nice ones can still be found today—although prices vary greatly from shop to shop.

Road map of Wyoming, ca. 1930s, from the Hotel Townsend.

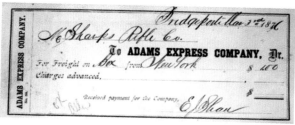

Adams Express Co. receipt from Sharps Rifle Co., for $1, March 3, 1876. (Hake's Americana, York, PA)

Left: Advertising brochure for Glidden barbed-wire fence, full color, ca. 1880.

Civil Defense pamphlet for
CONELRAD, 1953.

Die-cut can-shaped pamphlet for dog food,
full color, 3 3/4" x 6 1/4", ca. 1950s.

Above Right: American Cancer Society anti-
smoking bookmark, 1979, 2" x 7".

Right: *The Bonfire Of The Vanities* promotional
bookmark, 1988, 3 1/3" x 7 1/4".

Billhead, Planters Nut & Chocolate Co., black type and red logo, 7" x 7 3/4" dated 1937 . . . .$18

Billhead, J. Stevens Arms & Tool Co., 1895, rifle replacement, brown and white . .$5

Booklet, Cracker Jack Riddles, 2 3/4" x 5", 32-page premium published by Rueckheim Bros & Eckstein, back cover of The Home of Cracker Jack factory, some repairs, ca. 1910 . . . .$210

Booklet, Tips for Housewives From Gold Dust, 3 1/2" x 6", illustrated with 16 pages of cleaning tips, late 1930s $15

Booklet, Hires Happies, children's publication for Hires Household Extract, 3 1/2" x 5" full color, 12 pages, cartoon characters, ca. 1920s $18

Booklet, A. Hoff supply store, early 1900s, for record keeping, pocket-sized, mint .$5

Booklet, JELL-O, Polly Put the Kettle On, 1923, Maxfield Parrish cover $48

Booklet, Kellogg's Story Book of Games, part of series, 8 pages in color, 10" x 8", good condition, 1931 . . . . $7

Booklet, P. Lorillard, guide to pipe smokers, 1892, black and white $18

Booklet, Mogul Federal, connecting rod service, 1934, record keeping, pocket-sized $3

Booklet, Purina's Grand Old Opry souvenir album, 9 1/2" x 12 1/2", full-color cover, 24 pages featuring Eddy Arnold, 1945 . . . .$20

Booklet, Sunoco Oil Disney characters, 8 pages with Mickey, Donald, and Goofy, every page illustrated, clean, copyright Sun Oil Co., 1938 . . . .$135

Booklet, Winter Outings on Summer Seas, P & O Steamship Co., 32 pages with photos and map of trips to Cuba, ca. 1910, very fine $25

Booklet, die-cut, Rival Dog Food, can-shaped, ca. 1950s, full color $2

Booklet, die-cut, Wilbur's Cocoa, container-shaped, ca. 1930s, artist Maud Tousey Fangel, full color $2

Bookmark, anti-smoking, American Cancer Society, 1978, 2" x 7" $1

Bookmark, *Bonfire of the Vanities* novel, depicts author, 1988, 3 1/2" x 7" $1

Bookmark, Easy Dye, 1890, Victorian woman, full color $5

Brochure, In Case of Attack, 1953, Federal Civil Defense Administration, red, white, and blue $3

Brochure, Glidden barbed-wire fence, ca. 1880, Elwood & Co., DeKalb, Ill., full color $25

Brochure, Kodak photography contest, rules and prizes, 3" x 6 1/2", bright yellow background, some wear, early 1900s $45

Brochure, The World Famous Houdini: The Creator of the Handcuff King Act and Only Legitimate Jail Breaker, four pages, Victorian Theater, New York, 1912 . . . .$200

Box/container, Cracker Jack box, red, white, and blue waxed paper covering, end flaps missing, 3" x 6 1/2", browning and wear, early 1900s $54

Box/container, Borden's Cottage Cheese container, 5" circular, waxed cardboard with Season's Greetings and holiday illustrations of Beauregard, original lid, ca. 1960s $22

Box/container, Kellogg's cereal box with Tony the Tiger, 1957, promoting Admiral TV set prize $105

Box/container, Old Fashioned Mother's Oats, round cardboard, full color $9

Box/container, Post Sugar Crisp cereal box, 1958, promoting Mighty Mouse . . .$85

Check, Pejepscot National Bank, Brunswick, Maine, to National Bank of Redemption, Boston, 1886, printed in blue with textile industry theme vignette of woman with bolts of cloth, extremely fine $6

Coloring book, McDonald advertising/promotion, Ronald McDonald Goes to the Moon, copyright 1967, 12 pages, some creasing, fine $98

Cookbook, Federal Electric Range operating instructions and cookbook, 1929, orange cover $4

Container, Donald Duck, Sunshine Straws, orange box $18

Coupon card, Coca-Cola, child at grocery, full color, ca. 1930s $6

Display, Black Label beer, advertising cardboard airplane, multicolored, 12", ca. 1950s $35

Envelope, Cuyer gallery of photography, 1904, used in direct mail $2

Flyer, Lionel toy trains, orange and black with trains and accessories, 10" x 14", near mint, 1954 . . . .$15

Flyer, White Hickory Wagon Co., aprx. 8" x 10", ca. 1910 . . . . $6

Handbill, Drop Dead, repeating alleged President Ford message to New York City, hand-sized, reverse "We Need Carter," 1976 presidential campaign $6

Handbill, Gene Autry in *Mule Train*, Western movie, 1940s, single color $10

Handbill, public sale, 1947 farm auction, black type on yellow paper, 10" x 5 1/2" $2

Label, Amsterdam Broom Co., early 1900s, 3 1/4" x 4 3/4", full color $3

Label, On Rush Melons, Arizona fruit crate label, three colors $4

Label, Statue Brand, California bartletts, 1927, full color $22

Label, Uncle Sam Brand, Yakima Valley Apples, Wapato Fruit & Storage Co. . . .$35

Leaflet, World War II propaganda, prepared by Allies urging German people to free themselves from Nazi ring, 4" x 3", block printing in German, blue on white paper $5

Letterhead, Wrigley Company of Chicago, ca. 1920s, full color $12

Needle booklet, Farmers Fertilizer Co., ca. 1920s, unused $4

Needle booklet, Gambles Home Guard Paint, 1930s, die-cut can, green and white .$5

Needle booklet, Hygeia Coffee, 1925, black and white, pocket-sized $4

Pamphlet, Borden's Instant Coffee, Elsie the Cow on glossy paper cover, 3 1/2" x 4 1/2", copyright, ca. 1960s $10

Pamphlet, Your Guide To Disneyland, 3 1/2" x 8", issued by Bank of America, with color map, copyright 1955 . . . .$58

Receipt, Adams Express Co.. 1876, from Sharps Rifle Co., New York $40

Recipe booklet, Dilling's Marshmallows, 1920s, pocket-sized $2

Recipe booklet, JELL-O with George Washington cover, 4 1/2" x 6", 16 pages, 1924 . . . .$13

Recipe pamphlet and coupon, Betty Crocker, 1935 foods men rave about, series no. 4 . . . . $2

Road map, Hotel Townsend, 1930s, Wyoming, street scene, blue and white $30

Road map, Phillips 66, Minnesota 1935, with airplane $20

Road map, Wadhams (Red Horse), Wisconsin 1936, multicolored $20

Wrapper, Ivory Soap, early 1900s, Proctor & Gamble, green and white wax paper .$4

chapter fifteen

investing in
paper advertising

*"Now, there's three things you can
do in a baseball game. You can win,
or you can lose, or it can rain."*
Casey Stengel,
major league baseball manager

When one invests in paper advertising collectibles over a period of time, there are basically three possible outcomes—just like Casey Stengel's perception of baseball.

The idea in any investment is to win, of course. Barring that, the idea is not to lose; the theory being that your paper advertising collectibles at least maintain their value over the years and, thus, leave you with a little something to show for your efforts and expenditures.

Strange as it seems, we may well be on the brink of a great surge of personal investing in the United States, and this time around it does not center entirely on the stock market.

Some of us have felt that, in the midst of the great golden run of stocks, a lot of people were quietly buying antiques and collectibles for their own investment potential five, ten, or twenty years down the economic road. Unlike the process of the stock market, however, investing in antiques and collectibles is really not provable, or disprovable for that matter.

The high-road theory is that a small percentage of serious investors, once the stock market runs into another flat or extended decline period, will gradually shift part of their revenues to the glitter of objects from the past. The low-road theory holds, if you will, that significant numbers of people who have no regular dealings with stocks and bonds are regularly putting some of their extra cash directly into antiques and collectibles.

Whichever road is taken, the hope is to arrive at a future destination with something of value, and to enjoy the company of some paper treasures on the ride.

People have already figured out that if they spend $500 on a set of golf clubs, or $500 on a flower-patterned stuffed chair, they will have little of that "investment" remaining a decade from now. To be sure, the golf clubs might sell for a fraction of their original price at a garage sale in the future, and the chair would likely be donated to Goodwill or

In-store display sign for *Playboy* magazine; Jimmy Carter interview, 1976. Orange, black and white.

Paper advertising bag for Halloween treats with the Esso Tiger, ca. 1960s.

some other worthwhile organization.

Now suppose that same amount had been "invested," instead, in a scrapbook of Victorian advertising trade cards. At the time, it would have seemed more like a pleasure purchase—a good deal on a really nice group of colorful turn-of-the-century commercial cards in wonderful condition. Bear in mind, this is not Wall Street, but rather Main Street—simply obtaining some nice-looking old paper stuff to study, store and enjoy. The years go by and the single cards purchased, for an average of one or two dollars each, begin showing up in the marketplace at $6 to $8 each.

FIVE FACTORS OF VALUE:

1. *Quality.* From almanac to window sign, consider the design, proportions, message, coloring, and other details.

2. *Condition.* An item should be well-preserved, with no obvious damage. Raggedy paper collectibles will still be raggedy when you or your heirs eventually place them in the marketplace.

3. *Authenticity.* Documentation of a paper collectible's background is always a good idea. Gather some history. Perhaps its previous ownership (provenance) is also relevant. Was the old campaign poster President Richard Nixon's personal copy? Did the catalog of magic supplies once belong to the great Houdini himself?

4. *Rarity.* We eventually throw most paper away, especially paper with advertising printed on it. It was meant for a short life, and any paper advertising that survives, therefore, can be presumed to have some degree of rarity. Back in the 1960s, the Esso Oil Company distributed Halloween treat bags featuring their friendly tiger. The paper con-

Advertisement for Disney hats, *Walt Disney's Magazine*, 1957 issue. (Hake's Americana, York, PA)

tainers worked fine, but who bothered to save them—and how many weren't worn to shreds after a season or two?

5. *Name durability.* It is important to consider the importance of a paper advertising piece ten to twenty years in the future. Does it bear the image of a beloved company now secure in American commercial history? Or, is it a legend that generation after generation has grown-up with? Perhaps it represents Pumpkin Center's first joint-venture with McDonald's and ABC Television. Does that counter card promote Jimmy Carter's famous "lust in my heart" interview with *Playboy* magazine. Does the item bear the imprint of commercial legends such as Disney, Hershey's, Ford, RCA, and Campbell's—or does it involve famous persons and commercial endorsements like baseball's Stan Musial or aviation's Amelia Earhart? Maybe it promotes a product that will immediately spring to mind (and be appealing) to generations in the future, like Coca-Cola or IBM.

Clearly, there are advantages and disadvantages in investing in paper advertising collectibles, even when the amount spent is just an alternative to some other entertainment or household expense.

Here are some of the advantages:

• Aesthetic pleasure. You can display or decorate with them (avoid direct sunlight), bask in their unique history, and show them off to your friends.

• Modest marketplace. A majority of paper advertising may be purchased for a relatively modest amount. Some sports-related items are costly, and some political-related items bring heady amounts, but, for the most part, prices are reasonable. Many nice posters, almanacs, and even advertising catalogs cost less than the price of a best-selling hardback book or a couple of tickets to a first-rate movie.

• Groundfloor view. Unlike stamp collecting or even rare books, collecting paper advertising exclusively is a relatively uncrowded field. (Sure, there are a growing number of quality shows around the country featuring paper, but this is only the beginning.) Some experts see quite an opportunity here for collectors, and even investors, as the century turns.

• Mainly unpicked. With the possible exception of early almanacs and some trade cards, the vast majority of paper advertising collectibles remain unpicked and unclaimed by serious collectors and investors. A nice collection of most any category in this book can still be assembled by those willing to be diligent. Check out that box of junk in grandma's garage, the neighbor's yard sale, and the community flea market.

• Crossover potential. Whatever product paper advertising promotes is bound to have a developing crowd of collectors who eventually will be willing to "crossover" to add to their own holdings. Coke and McDonald's are, of course, two quick and easy examples. Other examples are dishware and glassware. A growing number of price guides on a specific ware are including the period advertisements (magazines and newspapers) which are also wonderful source material for the collection.

Amelia Earhart, in a 1928 magazine ad for Lucky Strike cigarettes. Earhart, however, did not smoke.

Here are some disadvantages:

• Retail prices. With most collectibles, those who give professional advice regarding investments will most always point out that you are buying at retail (from your favorite antiques dealer, for example) and will need to sell eventually at wholesale (say 50 percent of the price guide/retail price) to your favorite antiques dealer, for example. While this is not entirely true, it does give pause. What you pay initially is important, but paper advertising collectibles are everywhere, and frequently they can be found at a fraction of prevailing rates.

• Knowledge required. Yes, it ultimately pays to be informed; however, it is fair to assume that if a particular area of paper advertising is interesting in the first place, the typical collector will enjoy keeping informed as the years go by. Nevertheless, a learning experience is part of the investment.

• Expert advice. Clearly almost no one would suggest that you immerse a substantial part of your savings into collectibles. The experts know growth is much more substantial and reliable in stocks, bonds, real estate, precious metals, or probably even sow bellies. Follow the experts, of course, but save a few bucks for the fun of purchasing a few paper advertising collectibles which just might someday appreciate a little in value.

• Zero income. Paper advertising collectibles provide nothing in the way of income-producing assets, revenue, interest, dividends, or rent. This is still another good reason for avoiding making major investments in the field with "serious" rainy-day money.

• Market search. Even a really nice collection of paper advertising collectibles is not likely to sell door-to-door. As most people realize, you can usually unload stocks and bonds with a mere telephone call. Your trolley car advertising signs from the early 1900s may take quite a bit longer. Sale of major advertising pieces could take months, and dealing with a major auction house and waiting for the right auction sale could take six months or more.

Here are some suggestions, Robert's Rules if you will, for surviving and enjoying your stash of paper advertising collectibles:

Trolley car advertising sign for the J. M & I. Railroad in the 1890s; multiple colors.

• Condition is always important. Damage to an item through sunlight or sloppy handling can affect value. Protect your treasures and store them well.

• Provable connection with a famous person is great for your goods. If your Army recruiting poster was signed by General Omar Bradley, and came from the personal collection of General Norman Schwarzkopf, so much the better—but be sure to document it fully, and be sure you can prove it just as fully for a potential, but skeptic, buyer in the future.

• Seldom do paper advertising collectibles rapidly escalate in price. Years may go by without any significant change in value at all; however, it is not unreasonable in a typical economy for top-quality items to appreciate in the ten percent annual range over the long term.

• Paper advertising collectibles are a lot like love. When making a selection, bear in mind market appreciation could take a long time. If the time is spent with objects (or people) you really enjoy, it will pass in an amazing fashion. Moreover, the relationship itself will be enriching.

• Focus, if possible, on a particular period, subject or media. For example, transportation-related trade cards, nineteenth-century almanacs, Norman Rockwell calendars, or toy catalogs from the 1960s. Build a collection rather than an accumulation, it will probably appreciate at a better rate, and it certainly will look better in the marketplace.

Barbie trading cards poster, 1993, from Mattel. Full-color Fashion Play Cards.

Campaign booklet for the Kennedy 1960 presidential campaign.

Window card of Servais Le Roy and Flying Visit act, lithographed by Weller of London, ca. 1890s.

• Focus, II. Understand, as you go through the process, that some collectors acquire paper advertising items because of the historic design period they represent. For example, some unique and distinctive advertising emerged during the Art Nouveau period, roughly from 1895 until the outbreak of World War I. The Art Deco period, much more extensive, and seen in print in much larger numbers, ran from the end of World War I through the 1920s and into the 1930s.

• Never miss an opportunity to inform yourself about a particular area of paper advertising collectibles. Books, articles, shows, shops, dealers, advertisements, and collectors can all contribute to your knowledge.

• Never miss an opportunity, II. Be ever alert to opportunities to find quality paper advertising collectibles. Check out everything from garage sales to grocery stores, and places where uninformed people are cleaning out accumulations of paper. Chances are, at least some of them don't know what they are tossing away—and most of what you acquire, in such situations, will represent just about zero investment.

• Never miss an opportunity, III. Be willing to paw through stacks and boxes of material in antique malls and shops, and pay the price. (At no place will I ever recommend that you negotiate downward the price of a paper advertising collectible with a dealer—Never! Some dealers already operate on such a small profit margin that they could be really offended by the thought of such a practice. Never do it. But, does it hurt to ask if you qualify for any sort of discount?)

• Without a roadmap, proceed with caution. Unlike many other hobbies, or even areas of antique treasures, there is little developed information on the long-term future of paper advertising collectibles. Accordingly, the incidental, disposable, spendable, affordable dollar amounts are the best investment at the early level.

Considering all the points made thus far, there are still endless possibilities with paper advertising collectibles.

Many items are, in my opinion, under-priced, given their long-term interest, if they are actually priced at all. This would include most any paper advertising in good condition from the nineteenth century, and anything promoting Barbie, sports, automobilia, railroads, and television events. Also, watch for specialty catalogs (toys, tools, comic characters, etc.) from the 1970s and 1980s, and posters proclaiming social/cultural causes—no smoking, sales prohibited to minors, birth control, protect the environment, governmental service, and citizenship (including voting).

Product-related paper advertising which represents a low investment now, but which undoubtedly has long term name durability and possible future collectibility, include Chevrolet, Craftsman tools, RCA's "new" Nipper, Big Boy restaurants, Humble Oil characters, Kellogg's characters, Reddy Kilowatt (icon for electrical companies), McKid Clothing, and the tobacco industry's Joe Camel.

It might be also worthwhile to consider some of the so-called multiples in paper advertising—that is, items which could eventually appeal to two or more collector groups when you are looking for a buyer in the future. An example would be Lydia Pinkham's vegetable compound prod-

Cardboard sign message from an insurance company. Red and blue lettering, ca. 1950s.

Mailing insert, 3" x 5" color promo for pay-per-view world heavyweight fight.

ucts, popular at the turn of the century (of interest to those charting the rise of the women's feminist movement). Almanacs, like the *Graefenberg Light* or the *World Almanac* of the nineteenth century, will be appreciated by both almanac collectors and those with a fondness for old patent medications. Meanwhile, a John F. Kennedy campaign booklet from the 1960s could appeal to collectors of Kennedy political memorabilia, those with a taste for 60s nostalgia, and those with an affection for paper advertising in general.

In summary, obtain quality in the marketplace (or directly where it has been put to use), enjoy and preserve it, and be prepared to cash in during the latter innings.

chapter sixteen

future of the past: looking for the next paper advertising collectibles

When my youngest child was about eight years old, the entire family took a holiday trip to Churchill Downs, one of the country's most famous race tracks. The skies were sunny, the grounds were beautiful, and the horses were breathtaking to watch. According to our plan, everyone was entitled to select a favorite horse for a wager, but only for a few selected even-numbered races—or else this betting business would simply assume far too much importance.

Around the third race, little Matthew was tugging at my shoulder with a desperate request. "Let's pick Captain Action, Dad. He's gonna win and we'll win." Good ol' Dad explained that we were waiting until the next race, and, besides, this horse did not look all that great in the paddock. Moreover, the odds already posted reflected just how silly a choice it would be if we were to make the wager. "Aw, come on, Dad," he continued to plead, "This is really Captain Action's horse. He'll win in a walk. Honest." I, of course, repeated the firm and fatherly plan to wait until the next race, no matter how sure he was of a winner. Matthew continued pleading his case as the horse raced around the turns and won in a

Star Wars coloring box from Pizza Hut, 1997, 15" cardboard.

walk. This Captain Action paid about 90 to 1 on a two-dollar ticket, and the following day the newspaper noted the odds were the greatest for an eventual winner of the entire racing season at the legendary Churchill Downs.

Since that time long ago, two lessons have always remained with me: First, nobody, except maybe for eight-year-olds on sunny days, can actually predict the future. Second, never, ever, turn down a chance to bet on a horse named Captain Action.

No one knows exactly what kind of paper advertising will really be collectible in the future. If only we could gather up the neighborhood children, and ask them to please tell

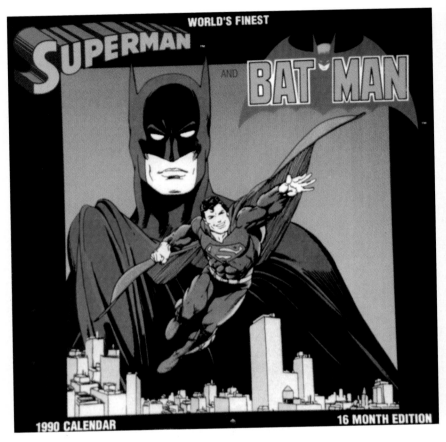

Superman/Batman calendar featuring classic comic book covers.
(Design Look Inc.)

Hershey's Halloween holiday standee, cardboard,
six feet tall, all color illustrated.

us what they will look back on and want to treasure when they are middle-aged. You
would get lots of answers, of course, but in reality the little folks have no idea what will
please them as old folks.

On the other hand, however, when I spotted the first pizza box with the *Star Wars*
image on it, I knew there just had to be some sort of future for paper advertising collectibles. Here was a giant *Star Wars* "coloring box" from Pizza Hut with the face of
Darth Vader boldly imprinted across the top. Wow! But who saved them? I don't know,
but probably not nearly enough to meet the demand a decade from now.

One beautiful fall day, my wife and I were wheeling our cart through the grocery
store when we almost collided with this great Halloween ghost standee from Hershey's.
It was over six feet tall, in beautiful color, holding armloads of Hershey's, Reese's
Peanut Butter Cups, Kit Kats, and Almond Joys. Another wow! This cardboard treasure
was not for sale because they were going to throw it out that day. Yikes! With permis-
sion from the store manager, we loaded the whole thing into the grocery cart and I gave
it a permanent home in my office.

Then, a few years ago, there was the 1990 combination Batman/Superman and other super heroes calendar in glossy color. Pow! Even after 18 months on the wall, I could not, and would not, throw it out. Surely a few more future generations will still love and collect these guys?

So, to conclude, we mere humans may have a limited capacity to predict what Captain Action will do next—but the potential to collect and enjoy these things of paper advertising seems boundless. So, ultimately, it comes down to just a couple of things:

First, bear in mind that much of today's advertising paper, whether a six-foot standee or a 15-inch square pizza box, is rapidly being discarded or recycled. Secondly, collectors who love Halloween, or Barbie, or McDonald's, or Batman, or Kellogg's, or Beth's Beautiful Flowers, or Moe's Car Wash will eventually come looking for paper memories of their favorite things.

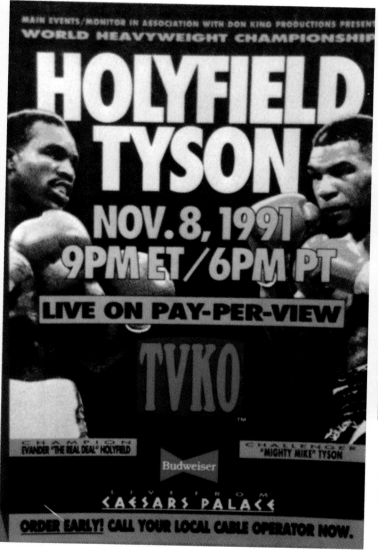

Specialized catalog for Halloween materials, 1997.

Mailing insert, 3" x 5" color promo for pay-per-view world heavyweight fight.

resources page

Auctions:

Cohasco Inc., Postal 821, Yonkers, NY 10703, historical document mail
  bid auction and sales.

Cerebro, P.O. Box 327, East Prospect, PA 17317, tobacco ephemera auctions.

Hake's Americana & Collectibles, P.O. Box 1444, York, PA 17405, mail and phone
  memorabilia and advertising auctions.

Leland's Collectibles, Inc., 245 Fifth Ave., New York, NY 10016, sports
  memorabilia auctions.

Skinner, Inc., 63 Park Plaza, Boston, MA 02116, auctioneers and appraisers.

Swann Galleries, Inc., 104 East 25th St., New York, NY 10010, auction gallery.

Books:

Advertising, Confident Collector series, by Dawn Reno (Avon Books).

American Illustrator Art, by Anne Gilbert (House of Collectibles).

Complete Book of Small Antiques and Collectibles, by Katherine McClinton (Bramhall
  House).

The Directory of 19th Century British Illustrators, by Simon Houfe
  (Antique Collector's Club).

The Directory of 20th Century British Illustrators, by Alan Horne (Antique
  Collector's Club).

Hake's Guide to Advertising Collectibles, by Ted Hake (Krause Publications).

Huxford's Collectible Advertising, 3rd edition, by Sharon and Bob Huxford,
  (Collector Books).

Insider's Guide to Old Books, Magazines, Newspapers and Trade Catalogs, by Ron
  Barlow and Ray Reynolds (Windmill Publishing).

Letterheads, 100 Years of Great Design, 1850-1950, by Leslie Cabarga,
  (Chronicle Books).

Paper Collectibles, the Essential Buyer's Guide, by Robert Reed (Krause Publications).

Petretti's Coca-Cola Collectibles Price Guide, by Allan Petretti (Antique Trader Books).

Petretti's Soda Pop Collectibles, by Allan Petretti (Antique Trader Books).

Posters, Confident Collector series, 2nd edition, by Tony Fusco (Avon Books).

Tobacco Advertising, the Great Seduction, by Gerald Petrone (Schiffer Publications).

Victorian Trade Cards, by Dave Cheadle (Collector Books).

Warman's Paper, by Norman Martinus and Harry Rinker (Krause Publications).

Publications:

Antique & Collectibles, P.O. Box 13560, El Cajon, CA 92022

Antique Corridor, P.O. Box 602, Greenfield, IN 46140

Antique Gazette, 6979 Charlotte Pike, 106, Nashville, TN 37209

Antique Shoppe, P.O. Box 2175, Keystone Heights, FL 32656

Antique Shopper, 37600 Hill Tech Dr., Farmington Hills, MI 48331

Antique Traveler, P.O. Box 656, Mineola, TX 75773

Antiques Today, 977 Lehigh Circle, Carson City, NV 89705

Arizona Antique News, P.O. Box 26536, Phoenix, AZ 85058

Cape Cod Antiques & Arts, Box 39, Orleans, MA 02653

Carter's Promotions Pty. Ltd., Locked Bag 3, Teffey Hills, NSW 2084, Australia

Cochrands Art Antiques & Collectible, 121 McBrown Rd., Petaluma, CA 94952

Collector's Corner, 2800 East 1st Ave., Vancouver, BC V5M 4S9, Canada

Collectors Journal, P.O. Box 601, Vinton, IA 52349

Collectors News, P.O. Box 156, Grundy Center, IA 50638

Cotton & Quail Antique Trail, P.O. Box 326, Monticello, FL 32345

Farm & Dairy Antique Collector Guide, P.O. Box 38, Salem, OH 44460

Flea Market Shopper, P.O. Box 8, Lahabra, CA 90633-0008

Hudson Valley Antiqer, 60 Mill Road, Rhineback, NY 12572

Indiana Antique Buyers News, P.O. Box 213, Silver Lake, IN 46982

Mt. States Collector, Box 2525, Evergreen, CO 80439

Old Stuff, P.O. Box 1084, McMinnville, OR 97128

Renningers Antique Guide, P.O. Box 495, Lafayette Hill, PA 19444

Rosie Wells Enterprises, Inc., R.R. 1, Canton, IL 61520

The Antique Shoppe of the Carolinas, 1226 Westmoreland Dr., Lancaster, SC 29420

The Auction Exchange, P.O. Box 57, Plainwell, MI 49080-0057

The Collector, P.O. Box 148, Heyworth, IL 61745

The Collector, 436 W. 4th St. Suite 222, Pomona, CA 91766

The Vintage Times, P.O. Box 7567, Macon, GA 31209

Treasure Chest, Box 245, N. Scituate, RI 02857-02245

Mid Atlantic Antique Magazine, P.O. Box 908, Henderson, NC 27536

Yesteryear, P.O. Box 2, Princeton, WI 54968

News Service:

Antique and Collectible News Service, PO Box 204, Knightstown, IN 46148, serving
more than 40 specialty publications. E-mail Acns@aol.com.

about the author

Robert Reed has written and published more than 500 articles on antiques and collectibles. He is a regular contributor to a wide range of publications from *Antiques Today* to *Yesterday*. This is his third book. A fourth book, on advertising bears and dolls, is underway. When not at work, Robert can be found at play with his four grandchildren—Megan, Beth, Mac, and Moe.